To Our Readers:

INTERNATIONAL

"The Book That Lies Flat"
— *User Friendly Binding* —

This title has been bound using state-of-the-art **OtaBind®** technology.

- The spine is 3-5 times stronger than conventional perfect binding
- The book lies open flat, regardless of the page being read
- The spine floats freely and remains crease-free even with repeated use

We are pleased to be able to bring this new technology to our customers.

Health Communications, Inc.

3201 S.W. 15th Street
Deerfield Beach, FL 33442-8190
(305) 360-0909

OTABIND®

INTERNATIONAL

The Netherlands

The Alternative 12 Steps:

A Secular Guide
To Recovery

MARTHA CLEVELAND, PH.D.
AND
ARLYS G.

Health Communications, Inc.
Deerfield Beach, Florida

Library of Congress Cataloging-in-Publication Data

Cleveland, Martha.
   The alternative 12 steps: a secular guide to recovery / by
Martha Cleveland and Arlys G.
     p.   cm.
   Includes bibliographical references.
   ISBN 1-55874-167-4
   1. Alcoholics — Rehabilitation. 2. Twelve-step programs.
I. G., Arlys. II. Title.
HV5278.C54 1991   91-9154
362.29′286—dc20   CIP

© 1992 Martha Cleveland and Arlys G.
ISBN 1-55874-167-4

Publisher: Health Communications, Inc.
          3201 S.W. 15th Street
          Deerfield Beach, Florida 33442-8190

Cover design by Andrea Perrine

·DEDICATIONS·

To my sons Peter and Vladimir Jr.

Arlys

· · · · ·

To my parents — who set my feet on the path.
To Walter — who has walked with me
every inch of the way.

Martha

(The Twelve Steps are reprinted and adapted with permission of Alcoholics Anonymous World Services, Inc. Permission to reprint and adapt the Twelve Steps does not mean that AA has reviewed or approved the content of this publication, nor that AA agrees with the views expressed herein. AA is a program of recovery from alcoholism — use of the Twelve Steps in connection with programs and activities which are patterned after AA, but which address other problems, does not imply otherwise.)

The Twelve Steps of Alcoholics Anonymous

1. We admitted we were powerless over alcohol — that our lives had become unmanageable. 2. Came to believe that a Power greater than ourselves could restore us to sanity. 3. Made a decision to turn our will and our lives over to the care of God *as we understood Him*. 4. Made a searching and fearless moral inventory of ourselves. 5. Admitted to God, to ourselves and to another human being the exact nature of our wrongs. 6. Were entirely ready to have God remove all these defects of character. 7. Humbly asked Him to remove our shortcomings. 8. Made a list of all persons we had harmed, and became willing to make amends to them all. 9. Made direct amends to such people wherever possible, except when to do so would injure them or others. 10. Continued to take personal inventory and when we were wrong promptly admitted it. 11. Sought through prayer and meditation to improve our conscious contact with God, *as we understood Him*, praying only for knowledge of His will for us and the power to carry that out. 12. Having had a spiritual awakening as the result of these steps, we tried to carry this message to alcoholics, and to practice these principles in all our affairs.

·CONTENTS·

·INTRODUCTION·

Martha

My name is Martha. The meeting is about to start. I stand in the circle with all the others, reaching out to grasp the hands of those on either side of me. The room is quiet. Then someone says, "God," and I deliberately and self-consciously remain silent. I can't speak to a god I don't believe in. Once "God" has been said, I fervently join with the others and finish: ". . . grant me the serenity to accept the things I cannot change, the courage to change the things I can, and the wisdom to know the difference." I squeeze the hands I am holding, release them and return to my seat. Once again the mysterious process has begun. The understanding, the undemanding love offered by AA and its affiliate groups takes over and a healing energy enters the room. But I am left with a nagging uneasiness.

For many years I have struggled with the residue of growing to adulthood with an alcoholic father. I have searched for self-esteem, for trustful intimacy, for peace. To the outer world I have appeared competent, confident and successful — but in my inner world I am still sometimes insecure, tentative and pushed to accomplish things that society praises, rather than things that would bring me pleasure and satisfaction.

The map that helps me most as I search for a serene self is the 12-Step program. It has become the cornerstone of my emotional growth and my spiritual life. Yet there is one big problem — and that problem is "God."

Millions of suffering people have had their lives healed by accepting the 12-Step program and the Judeo-Christian God that it seems to address, but their God is not my god. Nor is their God my higher power. Theologically I am an atheist. I don't believe in a traditional God or the Judeo-Christian dogma. Philosophically I am an agnostic. I believe the essential nature of things or ultimate causes, such as God, Jehovah or Allah, are simply unknowable. My higher power is not a singular entity to be addressed with a capital H and a capital P. So as I join this meeting, as I try to live by this program that is so important to me, I am constantly forced to translate and transform the program's words to meet my own personal beliefs. I feel set apart from the group. I feel different.

Arlys

My name is Arlys. I began the 12-Step program when my sons were nine and ten years old. I had tried and tried to be a good wife and mother, but nothing I did could fix our terrible problem. My husband drank. He drank in bars instead of coming home. Late at night he would finally come in, drunk, wanting to fight. Sometimes I fought with him, sometimes I drank with him. But most of the time I just tried harder to make things right.

I was ashamed, too ashamed to ask for help. A friend saw my pain and gave me some books on alcoholism. I read them, then hid them in my drawer under my nightgowns. They didn't seem to have the remotest connection to my family's special situation.

One day my son asked me a simple question. He asked, "Will Dad be home when my friends come for my party?" It was clear he was afraid Dad would embarrass him in front of his friends. The lid blew off my denial. I could hear at last that my husband's drinking was hurting my children. My love for them pushed me around the corner and started me on a new journey that took me to a 12-Step group.

I soon discovered that my problems and the problems of our family had as much to do with my own attitudes and behavior as with my husband's drinking. I turned my attention to myself and began to feel a new inner strength and calmness. Within months my husband reached for sobriety and began his own 12-Step program.

In my 12-Step journey I've covered a lot of ground. When I began, I was a religious person and full of my pain. In my process I've come nose to nose with myself many times. I've learned that I used alcohol inappropriately myself, that I was emotionally immature, that I carried unhappiness from my childhood. I also learned to be strong and to trust my own feelings and my own truth. And eventually, I faced my conflict with religion.

When I was six years old I knew there was no God. Instinctively I knew that God or no God made no difference. I accepted this truth as naturally as I knew the grass was green and felt cool and soft under my bare feet. I learned from my family and church that this attitude was wrong and bad, so I set about correcting myself. I became a sponge for religious indoctrination. I listened to what my church taught me. I tried to be good and do it right.

It wasn't until I came to the 12-Step program that I finally confronted my confused and conflicted beliefs about spirituality and religion. A small inner voice still told me there was no God. I listened and I believed.

I began the process of shedding God and my traditional religious beliefs. I examined what I was releasing and found many good and helpful ideas. But I couldn't let go of my atheistic truth. I couldn't let go of the Steps either — they worked for me. What to do?

I solved my problem by rewriting the Steps, leaving out references to God. It worked, and the program opened up for me. Rewriting the Steps gave me the freedom to work my program in a way that is vital and self-respecting. My Steps are truly my own.

A Map For The Journey

Years ago each of us began a journey. Our lives were in disorder and our minds were full of pain. So, like the men and women of the great myths, we each set out on a personal quest to find the treasure that would heal our lives. We tore ourselves away from past beliefs and behaviors. We left the familiar behind. Sometimes we crawled in terror, sometimes we walked with calm and sometimes we ran with exultation toward our goal. We overcame obstacle after obstacle — the trembling of fear, the nausea of hatred, the explosion of anger, the blindness of dishonesty, the immobility of confusion. Sometimes we retreated into weakness, only to go forward again with growing strength.

Gradually it has become clear to each of us that our journeys are different from the quests in the myths we read as children. Mythical quest journeys had clear goals and a clear ending point. But we will find no permanent solutions. Instead we are rewarded as our lives heal and we journey inward to the treasure of our honest selves. This can be true for everyone. Each man and woman can live a journey that is a heroic venture — each life can be a quest of importance and dignity.

This book is a map for anyone to use. But it is not a detail map or a topographical one. It is a map that only the person using it can understand — to others it may make no sense. It is to be followed within the context of each individual life. Each person's destinations will be unique, each person determines how far he or she will go and how long it will take. The important thing is to decide to take the trip. It starts with the First Step.

· CHAPTER ONE ·

What Is Your Suffering?

---

*I do not ask either your opinions or
your religion, but what is your suffering?*

Louis Pasteur

• • • • • •

One Man's Suffering Seeds A Miracle . . .

A man was alone with a terrible terminal disease. No one could help him and he couldn't help himself. He was an energetic successful New York stockbroker, but he knew his uncontrollable illness could wipe out his life.

Then, when he was afraid his disease might destroy him, the stockbroker met another man who had the same kind of sickness. The man he met was a physician from Akron, Ohio, who was in desperate need of help. The stockbroker's name was Bill, the physician's name was Bob and they both suffered from the disease that we today call alcoholism.

1

Bill wasn't sure he could help Bob, but he told Bob the story of his own struggle and the things he did to try to help himself. In this experience Bill discovered that the way to hold off his own disease was to try to help another affected person.

So Bill and Bob looked for others like themselves. They found them in hospitals and on street corners, at business meetings and dinner parties. Wherever they searched, they seemed to find men and women with the tormenting, inescapable, compulsive need to drink themselves into oblivion. Every one of them was addicted to alcohol.

Bill and Bob and the others formed self-help groups, first one in Akron and then one in New York City. The only requirement for belonging to a group was a sincere desire to remain free of alcohol. Together the group members experimented with methods that would help them stay sober. From their experiences Bill created a 12-Step program for living.

As time passed, more and more groups sprang up in different towns and cities across the country. They called themselves Alcoholics Anonymous, AA for short. "One day at a time" they followed the 12-Step program for recovery.

Today 12-Step groups help people recover from many kinds of compulsive behaviors. The 12 Steps help people all over the world heal their addictions to alcohol, compulsive eating and dieting, compulsive gambling and sexual activity, the emotional ravages created by growing up in an alcoholic family or the pain of living with an alcoholic spouse. This program, started when two frightened desperate men helped each other, has spread and spread. Millions of people have lived by its words and changed their lives. The 12 Steps really work.

. . . And The Miracle Can Work For Everyone

The original 12-Step program is a wonderful proven way of living. It heals. But some of us have a problem with the language. Some of us read the Steps and the words "God," "Him," "pray" and "Higher Power" don't fit into the way we believe. We see ourselves as non-religious people, and these words seem like religious words to us. We are told this is a spiritual program, not a religious one, that "any Higher Power is okay," but the capital H and the capital P suggest a deity, and any deity is not okay with us. *wrong* Some of us become so uncomfortable with this language that we reject the whole program. We throw out the baby with the bathwater. When we do this, we lose a wonderful chance to change and enrich our lives.

And so this book. As 12-Step practitioners, we believe in the 12-Step program. We believe it can work for anyone. Our objective is to help non-religious people accept the healing power of the Steps. This is the same program, same principles, same values, same scope, same depth — all of it said in a little different language. We have extracted the actions and principles of the original Steps and put them into a secular context. It's as if they were written in French and we didn't speak French very well, so we carefully translated them into our native Spanish. It simply makes it clearer for us, and it's easier to bring our own spiritual meaning to the 12-Step way of living. Whether a person believes in God, whether a person is Jewish, Christian, Mohammedan, atheist or agnostic, none of this matters. What does matter is that we learn to live the 12-Step way. It isn't important how we climb the mountain, as long as we commit ourselves to the journey.

· CHAPTER TWO ·

A Program For Living

What Is The 12-Step Way?

The title of this chapter says it all. The 12 Steps are a program for living, a program of action fueled by spiritual energy. Basically the Steps suggest a system of holistic healing — a practical system of action that integrates mind, body and spirit. When our mind, body and spirit are integrated, we approach life with a new attitude that leads to balance and contentment.

We believe the 12-Step program suggests a practical philosophy for each of us — a philosophy of living. We also believe this program needs to be kept separate from any religious implications. In order to work the Steps, what we think about God doesn't matter but what we believe about our own whole self does.

The 12 Steps are a working framework anyone can use to recover from personal turmoil and pain. There are no set concepts or dogma. Each person decides the program's meaning in a unique way. There are no leaders, no right way or wrong way, only our own way. We needn't compare our process or the way we work the program with anyone else's. Each person's interpretation is valid and life-enhancing for that person. And we don't even have to understand how or why it works. We just find that as we apply the Steps, our lives begin to change — and the change is good.

The 12-Step program focuses on self-examination and a connection with spiritual energy. It also encourages us to go beyond theorizing about our condition and to use the Steps as a specific, pragmatic, practical guide for recovery. It's not enough to think and reflect about our problems. As Bill W. said, *"The spiritual life is not a theory, we have to live it."* In other words, we must think about our situation and then physically, emotionally and spiritually act on it.

Maybe the reason the program is useful to so many different kinds of people is that it pulls together basically contradictory ideas. In order to carry out the Steps, we must make a personal individual choice to connect with spiritual resources greater than we are. We make a controlled, conscious choice to transcend the circumstances of our lives. At the same time, we seek help from a source of spiritual power outside of our own personal control and beyond our everyday consciousness. This contradictory nature of the 12 Steps allows the program to serve anyone, no matter what their religious or philosophical belief system.

How Do We Live The 12-Step Way?

Harmful compulsive behaviors or addictions are any thoughts, feelings or actions that mask our emotional pain and that we are unwilling or unable to change. They are the marks of our unhealthy self, our self-destructiveness. For many of us this kind of self-defeating behavior has been our way of coping with life's difficulties. The problem is that self-defeating behavior does just what it says: it defeats our self. Life gets more and more out of control, harder and harder for us to manage. This is where the 12 Steps can help.

We can't eliminate problems from our past, present or future, but the Steps can help us deal with what has been, what is now and what is to come. When we live as they suggest, we can stop letting pain and problems control us. We can learn to say no to what hurts us and yes to ideas, feelings and actions that help us.

We work the Steps with both our conscious and unconscious minds. We use our conscious minds when we read and study for greater understanding of our problems. We call a friend from the program when we are in trouble. We consciously examine a Step and think about how to apply it to our lives. With commitment and deliberation, we practice our new ways until they are a part of us.

We use our unconscious minds, too. We use them when we meditate, when we are absorbed in creative thought or work, when we dream. New ideas and feelings "come" to us; different solutions to our problems "appear" in our minds. We think about the Steps and our unconscious responds. Our conscious and unconscious energies flow back and forth, feeding on each other, stimulating each other, producing change and growth. Slowly, slowly they lead us to health and serenity.

When we carry out the actions suggested by the 12 Steps, we examine every part of our selves and our lives: our past, present and hopes for the future. We assess our true character and nature. We look at the experiences we've had and how we've reacted to them. We look at how we've played out our roles and we examine our creativity.

Working the Steps means that we examine each part of our selves and we look at the whole picture, too. In a way, each of us is like a kaleidoscope made up of many varied pieces — physical pieces, mental pieces, emotional pieces. All these pieces are in almost constant movement, resting only for a moment to form the unique picture that is us at that single instant in time. Then it changes to a new arrangement as life is lived and the scope is turned.

What Can The Program Do For Us?

The results of living the 12-Step way are wonderful. Here are some of the things that can happen for anyone who commits to the program and works at following it.

We Learn To Live Right Here, Right Now.

The Steps teach us not to spend our time living in the past or imagining the future. What was, was; what will be, will be. Our only chance for changing, growing and living well is in the present instant. Right now is the only moment we have to act on our lives. *The only moment we have.* Living in the here and now produces self-empowerment, which means we learn to change today, not to put it off. And we learn to take whatever we can from the present moment that will strengthen us.

Perhaps we glance up to see the sun shining through new spring leaves against a pale blue sky or look up from the evening TV and notice a full moon shining in through the window. We experience a moment of wonder and happiness at the beauty. This moment, this remembered image and the feeling that goes with it, can be stored in our memory bank to be retrieved and give us a feeling of peace when we are anxious or fearful.

We Learn To Respect Ourselves.

For many of us it's very hard to act on our own needs and feelings instead of blindly responding to the feelings and actions of the people around us.

It's hard to answer the phone and tell a friend, "I'm sorry, but I just can't talk now," when we are tired and there are a million things to do before dinner. It's hard to tell our neighbor we can't help him move this weekend because we're going to stay home and watch the football game.

It's difficult for many of us to respect ourselves enough to answer our own needs first. It doesn't feel right because our self-respect is so low. And even if we want to change our ways, we don't know how. But the Steps teach us. Gradually we learn to take care of our own fatigue before the needs of a friend. Gradually we learn to turn away the requests of another when we need time to ourselves.

We Learn To Detach From Others And Let Them Run Their Own Lives.

The 12 Steps teach us a lot about detachment. When we detach from someone, we separate from them emotionally. We separate with compassion and without anger. It's really just a matter of respect. We learn to respect other people enough to detach from trying to manage their lives or control their feelings. We learn to let others do what they do, think what they think, feel what they feel. We don't interfere by trying to change them, fix up whatever mess they get into or make them feel better or worse.

When our adolescent daughter gets into trouble at school, we express our interest, give her our support and let her repair the situation and take whatever consequences come. Detachment may sound cruel, but really it is respectful because it assumes she is strong enough and smart enough to handle her own affairs. We respect her enough to support her and, at the same time, stay out of her way to let her work out her own problems in her own way. We respect her enough to believe in her.

We Learn To Take Care Of The Child Within Us.

We each carry a child within us, the remnant of the little boy or little girl we once were. Those of us who are compulsive or addictive live with a frightened, angry little person deep in our unconscious minds. This child carries the pain that blocks our road to serenity.

The 12 Steps teach us to find, to know and to heal our inner child. We learn that we have created our present world out of our child's past. Today is not the past, and we no longer have to live by its rules. Today, as adults, we can speak to our inner child. We can choose which of our child's feelings, thoughts and beliefs are relevant and useful in our present life and which we can put away.

We Find A New View Of Reality.

Probably one of the most important benefits the 12-Step program gives us is a clearer view of reality. This doesn't mean we get the benefits without lots of effort on our part. As we live the 12-Step way, we break out of the web of denial, rationalizations, justifications, lies, pretenses and posturings that has created our present world.

Our reality is different when our view of life becomes less clouded and our concept of self becomes stronger. When we see more clearly and feel more confident, our life changes and we experience a reality that feels brighter and more honest. We can say, "The reason I didn't get the supervisor job is that I'm often late and sometimes take more than my hour for lunch. It's not because Judy buttered up the boss and he fell for it. I really wanted that job, and I'm going to have to change some things so I can get the next promotion." No excuses, no rationalizations, no justifications or pretenses — instead, a clear honesty and forthright purpose.

Our Relationships Change.

Our relationship to ourselves is the most important one. The program teaches us how to honor ourselves, how to become our own best friend. We learn to listen to ourselves, trust ourselves and know we won't ever let ourselves down. We truly believe we must have this kind of self-love and respect before we can have honest relationships with other people.

The program also gives us a structure to help us explore our relationships with others. In the past, even though we may have felt powerless, we often acted in powerful ways that hurt people around us. We controlled people by manipulating them. We yelled or clung or coldly turned away. We loved conditionally, and we alone set the conditions.

The Steps help us discover the pain we have caused and how to make amends for causing it. We learn we cannot control our relationships, we can only control ourselves within them. As a result, we can build respectful relationships. And in respectful relationships everyone gets better and better.

Finally the program teaches us how to work on the relationship between ourselves and our spiritual resources. This relationship provides great power for our healing, and it's a source many of us haven't used very well. The Steps teach us to stop assigning power only to the conscious control of our thinking mind. They encourage us to be open to healing energy from all kinds of internal and external sources. Each of us can find spiritual connections that are uniquely ours. Then we never have to feel alone in the world — our own spiritual supports are always available to us.

The Journey Is Our Own

It seems that once we start to walk the 12-Step path, we are in recovery from self-abuse. Each of us instinctively does what we need to do to heal. Our spirit strengthens our healthy self, and our self-destructive self begins to disappear. But it's slow. It takes time for our changes to work deep into the fabric of our lives.

Real growth may appear as insignificant happenings, tiny things done differently, minute alterations in the way we respond. There is no sudden, dramatic high — we are never magically "healed." Many of us will make recovery a life-long adventure. We must be patient, generous and loving with ourselves. We must learn to celebrate our small successes. Small changes add up to real healing and growth as we move toward self-acceptance and self-love.

Our addictions and compulsions are negative processes. Some of us suffer from severe addictions to alcohol and drugs, gambling, overeating, undereating or sex. Some of us are controlled by chronic obsession, resentment, anger, anxiety or problem relationships. Whether they threaten our lives or our spirits, any of these processes can act as an insulating cloak around us — a dark, thick shroud that has no openings. We are suffocating in a burial gown we have made for ourselves, and we are blind to new ways that might help us rip open its seams.

Beginning to work a 12-Step program is a way to pick up our own personal seam ripper. With it we can cut a small hole in our shroud. We push first a finger, then a hand, then our whole arm through the opening and become connected with what can heal us. We find hope and strength. We find new ways to make connections with our selves and with our world.

Eventually we will have many holes in the seams of our shroud. They will be big enough to step through, so we move outside and stand in the world with full spiritual vision. We can take our rightful place, a place of peace and respect. We will be truly alive. We will move from resentment to acceptance, from self-pity to gratitude, from fear to trust, from dishonesty to honesty and from confusion to serenity. It's a long, hard trip, but it's a journey anyone can travel.

A statement often read at the opening of 12-Step meetings goes like this: "The 12-Step program is a spiritual program, based on action, coming from love." This means the Steps are based on practical work and action. It also means the energy of love for ourselves, for others and for the connection with countless spiritual resources leads to our ever-expanding spirit. The Steps are not static. Their meaning for us changes as we change. Then we change in relationship to their changed meaning. It's in this interplay between Step and self that emotional and spiritual healing happens, and serenity becomes an active force in our lives.

CHAPTER THREE

Step 1

Admit we are powerless over other people,
random events and our own persistent negative
behaviors, and that when we forget this,
our lives become unmanageable.

Principles: Insight, Honesty

· · · · · ·

S tep 1 is a shift in thinking. We shift from thinking that we are powerful and in charge of our
lives to accepting the reality that our efforts
haven't worked. Our struggles to control ourselves
and others have only made our lives unmanageable.
In this way we have been blind to ourselves. Step
1 gives us the insight and honesty to admit that we
are not managing our lives very well, that a lot of
things are beyond our control and that we live

with emotional pain. It is the first step on our road to serenity. We can begin to use the affirmation of serenity that millions of people have used before us.

Today I seek the serenity
To accept the things I cannot change,
The courage to change the things I can,
And the wisdom to know the difference.

(Adapted from "The Serenity Prayer," by Reinhold Niebuhr)

Something About Denial And Self-Deception

Unexamined lives are often lives lived in denial. Denial is not conscious lying — it is simply self-deception, a series of personal blind spots. We don't have to be bad people or have bad problems in order to engage in self-deception. The only requirement is that we don't want to know all the truth about ourselves or our lives. We use our wonderfully complex brains to deny and obscure reality and to keep on believing that we are managing, that we are in control.

We throw ourselves into arranging the outcome we desire. And the outcome we desire is to keep on doing what we are doing. We want to feel good about ourselves without facing the pain and difficulty of admitting that we aren't able to control other people, the random events around us and even our own persistent negative behavior. We want to feel good about ourselves without having to change, and denial is our shortcut.

We have many ways of deceiving ourselves. We deny that we have a problem. We hide a problem behind a visible asset or success. We give our problem a new name. We manipulate or blame others. We control. We knock ourselves out to please, to be good. We bully. We act helpless. We rationalize and justify. The list goes on and on in endless variation.

Our techniques are mental inventions that deny the truth about ourselves. We believe our inventions and cling to them. The denial that has been our shortcut becomes our dead end. We are blocked from real growth because we are blind and we stay blinded. Blindness remains our condition until we are ready to grow up.

Our Inner Condition Makes Us Ready For Step One

We have problems. Whatever they are, however large or small, we are afflicted and affected and less than serene. It's a chronic situation. Some of us are stuck with an insolvable problem, some with a generalized inner distress. Our problems may be at the crisis stage or they may not be terribly serious. They may be obvious to outsiders or others may hardly notice them. It doesn't matter. The point is that we feel an inner strain. Emotionally and perhaps physically, we are not comfortable.

Our chronic problems often grow up around points of unresolved pain. We have hurts from the past and we attach to them strong emotions, such as rage, feelings of inferiority or fears of being excluded or abandoned. We pile these emotions on top of each other and are propelled into ways of behaving that cause us even more pain. So we fall into a vicious cycle of compulsive feelings and activities as our solution.

We Are Packed Full Of Self And Loaded With False Power

One thing true of most of us is that we are full of ourselves. We are tied up in our own knots — we have no objectivity about what we think, feel or do. We are full of our pain and our rigid view about ourselves, other people and our problems. We are full of confusion, resentment, blame, anger, self-justification and self-pity. We can't realistically see our own part in our problems because we can't realistically see ourselves. We are unable to see, stop or control what we do that causes us so much pain. The weaker we feel, the more powerful we try to be — and the more powerful we try to be, the more we fail. It goes like this:

1. We can't see what the real problem is.
2. We can't see any solutions except those that come from our own confusion.
3. We take our confused solution and act on it compulsively again and again.
4. It doesn't work. Or it may work for a while, but eventually it will fail and things will go back to the way they were before we tried to fix them.
5. We do this dance again and again.

In this tight, closed little system, we attach ourselves to our problems and our method of fixing them. We attach to substances, activities and other people. We numb ourselves with drugs or alcohol. We drug ourselves with responsibility and compulsive overwork. We gamble. We overeat. We devote ourselves to rescuing others. We worry without ceasing, we hold resentments and are jealous. We become helpless and make others take care of us or we form abusive relationships to act out our low self-worth. We can't stop or control what we are doing. We can't stop because our negative attachments run deeper than our willpower can reach.

All of this inner distress puts down roots that grow and spread inside of us and our denial protects these roots. This means we continuously tend and reinforce that which weakens us. We don't ever let the roots dry out and shrivel. Instead we water them with our life's energy, the same energy we could use to form a happy relationship with life, with ourselves and with others.

Our Lives Become Unmanageable

Our lives become unmanageable because we have to believe that we are powerful; we have to believe we are in control. We *need* to be in charge. To feel a loss of personal power feels like a loss of self. We deny this loss of self/power by controlling for dear life. We think all we need to do is to keep on doing the same things we've been doing and do them harder. *Then* we will find a different outcome, a cure, a genuine happiness. We will do almost anything to be happy, anything but change ourselves — so our unhappiness continues.

An honest examination shows how "unmanaged" things really are.

• • • •

After my husband and I have a fight, I'm always the one who has to initiate getting back together. I've told him and told him I'd like him to start things sometimes, but he never, never does.

For one of the few times in my life I thought things were really under control — everything was going along just right. Then I had that awful car accident and everything fell apart. I was out of work for six months and couldn't do a thing about it.

When my boss criticizes something I've done, I always feel like a punished kid — I get mad and he gets irritated and turns me off. Everyone tells me this is crazy, and I know it gets in the way of a promotion, but I can't seem to change the way I feel or the way I act either.

• • • •

When we honestly examine our lives, we see unmanageability everywhere. It can be seen in our behaviors, such as irresponsibility or compulsivity. It shows in our strained relationships with others. We feel emotions that we can't control: rage, loneliness, chronic sadness or a need to be distracted by work, excitement or chaos. We find ourselves in a financial, legal, or job-related mess, and we can't get out. We war with the people we love and can't come to peace with them. In so many ways, large and small, seen and unseen, our lives are unmanageable. But most of us are slow to admit to our problem behaviors and our powerlessness to fix them.

Step 1 Is A Step Forward — One Step Back From Self

With Step 1, we go forward far enough to step back from ourselves and see that all our efforts and solutions have not helped. We are still the way we do not want to be. Denial has kept us stuck, but with Step 1 we at least become aware of our denial. We become aware that our efforts to control have kept us stuck. With fresh honesty we admit there is something wrong with the way we are living.

Step 1 gives us insight that cuts through our excuses, our rationalizations, our justifications, our blame — in other words, through our denial. It cuts right to the heart of the problem. As Walt Kelly's cartoon character Pogo said, "We has met the enemy, and he is us."

Step 1 shows us we have been fighting against ourselves, not for ourselves. We let go of the belief that we are managing well. We shift from thinking that we are powerful and in charge to believing in a new reality.

We Admit Our Powerlessness And Amazing Things Happen

All power is seductive. Giving up the illusion of power is as difficult and as wretched as giving up real power. We hang onto it as long as we are able. And our illusion of self-power corrupts us as absolutely as brute power corrupts a dictator. All of this changes when we accept the message of the First Step. We "admit we are powerless over other people, random events and our own persistent negative behavior . . .."

To admit our powerlessness means to give up and admit that we are spiritually depleted, emotionally exhausted from trying to fix problems we can't fix. We simply cannot manage any longer. Whatever power we did have is used up and we have nothing left to use or lose. Coming to accept all this is a giant leap toward self-honesty and truth. When we do, we begin to experience the paradox that accepting our powerlessness becomes the basis for ever-increasing spiritual strength.

As we let ourselves experience powerlessness, we feel it in our body and inner spirit. We feel lighter, more relaxed, as though we are yielding to new joy and energy and as though somehow we can rest. We feel more in tune, more connected with everything around us. To experience powerlessness is to be one with life instead of one against life.

Our potential to heal is tied to our understanding of the following:

1. What is within our power
2. What is beyond our power
3. Where we can join with wider powers.

When we understand this, we have the spiritual energy to face and walk through the pain we have worked so hard to deny and manage. When we admit powerlessness, we see choices where once we couldn't see any way out. We gain freedom in our thoughts, emotions and behavior. We find we actually have a lot of power to change ourselves, but only ourselves. This is different from the tight, self-controlling power of the past. This is real power based in honesty and true understanding. Real power can't be achieved, only accepted.

And this is when amazing things happen. When we stop trying to manage and control our problems, we mysteriously stop doing the things that are causing us the trouble.

This is true when alcoholics stop trying to manage their drinking and when worriers stop trying to manage their worries. When we resign from managing the problems of others, the situation may continue but the problems we make for ourselves disappear. We stop fighting for a new outcome. We simply let go of our interfering interest and control. We just quit. We don't try to figure it all out, we detach.

We let go of the things we can't manage and practice constructive self-management through working the Steps. And when we do, we find a life we lost when we became consumed with managing things that can't be managed.

Helen

Helen is a perfect person. She is married to Mr. Right and has three school-age children. She is competent and well-liked and her friends look up to her as a kind of superwoman. Helen is terrific and her life looks wonderful.

All the time she was growing up, Helen's father was erratically employed and abusive to her and her brothers and sister. Her mother was emotionally absent and neglectful. The household was chaotic. Helen vowed that when she grew up, she would never live like that.

She never did. Instead, the grown-up Helen became perfect. She was controlled and clean and graciously warm. She was everything she thought a wife and mother should be. Her husband was a nice, normal guy who provided a good living. Her son and two daughters were precocious, and she raised them by the latest child-rearing methods. Helen was proud of her children's accomplishments and she pushed them to achieve more.

Her family behaved as she directed, the way they ought. Secretly Helen felt superior. She had conquered her childhood. Under her surface warmth and graciousness she had a hidden contempt for people who lived in what she called "grubbiness."

Trouble began when her oldest child, Eric, was in junior high. He started making friends who were not up to Helen's standards. Eric wasn't clean, wore sloppy clothes and ate when he was hungry. He even started skipping school — Helen got calls from the principal's office. Eric wouldn't listen to her when she tried to talk to him nor would he listen to his father.

Helen was overcome with anxiety and thought Eric's future was at stake. She nagged and snooped and continued to try to mold him into her image. She felt like part of her life was reeling and she tried desperately to reassert her control.

Eric stood firm about his new-found independence, so Helen moved on and tightened her grip in other areas. She began giving her husband lists to remind him of things she wanted him to do. She over-scheduled her daughters with sports, lessons and academically-enriching activities. She doubled up on her high-profile volunteer work and gave lovely dinner parties at least twice a month. Life was still as perfect as Helen could make it.

Then Helen's husband had business reverses. She was outwardly kind and supportive but inwardly raging. How could he upset her life like this? How could she buy the things she needed? What would happen to the family? She began to monitor his business closely, to make suggestions and to "help" him. She organized and planned. Her neck hurt. She was exhausted.

Helen began to clean her house obsessively. She cleaned and cleaned. She cried with self-pity as she scrubbed floors on her hands and knees. She didn't know why she cried. She didn't even know why she scrubbed the floors.

One evening after Helen had done the dinner dishes, she returned to the kitchen and saw a banana peel lying in her immaculate sink. A boundless rage rose up from somewhere deep within her. She grabbed the banana peel and, waving it in front of her, stormed around screaming, "Who did this? Who did this?" Her family was stunned.

Helen couldn't stop. She stormed and screamed and raved. She knocked over a chair and even pounded the wall. Then she collapsed on her bed and sobbed for hours. The pain of her past came through her tears. She understood that her anger had nothing to do with a banana peel. Her anger had come from somewhere deep inside herself. She was frightened and realized that she had always been frightened. She was afraid to love and afraid of not being loved. She felt unsure of who she was. She felt empty inside. In a few seconds of clean honesty she understood the depth of her unhappiness and she understood that she was powerless.

Although she didn't know it, this moment was Helen's big turning point, her first Step 1. A few days later she went with a friend to a 12-Step group and began to live in a new way.

Helen had many insights as she began to work the Steps. She came to understand that her solution to her pain had been to become perfect. Striving toward perfection had made Helen feel powerful, the exact opposite of how she had always been afraid of feeling. Playing the game of Mrs. Perfect and winning had actually made Helen a loser in her own life. Helen began her 12-Step journey the night of the banana peel. She accepted her powerlessness and walked through her pain, past her perfection and into her own rich humanity.

Jerry

Jerry was only able to admit his problem in detox. Until then he tried to manage and control his alcohol and drug use by mental inventions, by denying he had a problem.

His attachment to booze and drugs began when he was 15. Life was a party and life was fun. Using gave him the emotional easiness he lacked and he loved it. He felt clever when he smoked and virile when he drank. Together they were a real high.

Sometimes Jerry acted inappropriately when he used, and sometimes he couldn't remember what he did. This didn't always happen, though, so he could pretend it was no big deal. He just remembered how good the booze made him feel and he couldn't wait until the next time.

Jerry started to use other drugs, too. When he was 19, he got in with a new crowd who used LSD and coke. They hung out together, went in together to make big buys and looked on each other as real friends.

Jerry's brother was concerned about him and talked about what awful effects drugs could have. Jerry was sure his brother was over-reacting and trying to control him. He was furious. This gave him a good reason to go to his friends and have a really great party.

Jerry continued to use different kinds of drugs, always trying for that perfect state of emotional ease he had found when he first smoked and drank. Most of the time he missed the mark and felt good for a while and then awful. Sometimes he just felt awful. He lost his third or fourth job and had to go to work as a bag boy at a supermarket. Jerry was always full of rage and resentment so he just used more drugs. He never connected his misery with his use.

His brother talked to him again about drugs, so Jerry decided to prove that he didn't have a problem. He actually quit using for almost six months. His health improved, his mind cleared and he got a better job and paid his overdue bills. His experiment in quitting "succeeded," so he began using again.

In a matter of weeks Jerry was out of control. He used all kinds of drugs and he used them all the time. He still tried to manage his behavior and made all sorts of rules, but he never carried through.

When Jerry wasn't invited to the family Thanksgiving dinner, his ever-present resentment erupted into a four-day high. He passed out in the hall of his apartment building, and his landlord had him taken to detox. Jerry was enraged and humiliated. He told the detox staff that he didn't need to be there, that he was a social user and his landlord caught him at a "bad time." The sideways glance one staff member gave another said it all — Jerry wasn't fooling anyone.

In Narcotics Anonymous Jerry finally stopped fooling himself. He acknowledged that his life was a mess and that drugs and booze were the reason. He practiced Step 1 with the profoundly simple idea that, since he couldn't conquer or manage his use, he would no longer try. He admitted powerlessness and started on the long road to being straight.

In his recovery Jerry healed many areas of his life that had been painful long before he started using. His resentment subsided. He learned to respect himself and others. Jerry grew up and found emotional ease without drugs.

We Begin At The Bottom

Connecting with real power begins in the ashes of our defeat, our admission of powerlessness. This is a place we have worked very hard to avoid. It takes honesty, courage and humility to accept this new start. But from defeat we can connect with life's fresh energy and rise with real power, real purpose and real inner strength. It is natural and uncomplicated. All we have to do is let go and accept that we are not ultimately in control. It takes practice, but soon we know this is a happier way to live. We forget our powerlessness sometimes, but when we do, we collect ourselves and start again. Life is forgiving and life's spiritual energy has no rules. It is available to us all, just because we are alive.

Admit we are powerless over other people, random events and our own persistent negative behaviors, and that when we forget this, our lives become unmanageable.

Today I will find ways to influence my life, while admitting I can't control the outcome of my actions.

I disagree with this.

· CHAPTER FOUR ·

Step 2

Came to believe that spiritual GoD
resources can provide power for our
restoration and healing.

Principles: Hope, Faith

· · · · · ·

The Second Step builds on the First. It asks us to go beyond admitting our personal power-lessness, to accept that there are powerful spiritual resources that can help us reshape our lives. All we have to do is to recognize, accept and connect with them. In Step 1 we acknowledge that we aren't in total control, that our individual power is limited. Step 2 tells us we can use spiritual re-sources beyond our own ordinary personal power to restore and heal ourselves.

25

Spiritual Resources — To Each His/Her Own

Lots of us confuse spirituality and religion. The words are often used interchangeably and we must realize that they shouldn't be, for they have different meanings. To call religion spiritual is true, but religion is only one source of spiritual power. There are many, many others.

The word *spirit* comes from a Latin word that means *breath, life, vigor.* We call something spiritual when it represents life or when it enhances life.

There are people who center their spirituality on religious practices and principles. There are others who find spiritual connections with things totally outside of any religious framework. As far as spirituality is concerned, to believe in a God or not to believe in a God doesn't matter. What matters is to have faith in our spiritual selves — in other words, to have faith in the energy that gives us life.

The phrase "spiritual resources" can be interpreted in many ways. Does it have to mean something great and mystical? Probably not. Does it mean there are a certain number of clearly-defined sources of power that we can tap into? No. There are many sources of spiritual power, more than any of us will ever be aware of or be able to use.

Spiritual power comes from whatever gives us peace, hope or strength and enhances our humanity.

The Higher Power of the original 12 Steps is a spiritual idea. A Higher Power can be a God or another kind of symbol. It can be goodness, love, a friend or an idea. It can be our own intellectual curiosity. It can even be the 12-Step program itself.

When we open ourselves to the power of spiritual resources, we open ourselves to an abundance of help that is beyond our comprehension. Each of us will find different powers, and those we use may change from day to day.

Some of us will reach out to nature, some to the calm, ordered events of everyday living. Some of us will find energy in the support of another person or the wise words in a book. Some of us will become healed by connecting with the deepest parts of our own nature, our internal wiser self. The sources of spiritual power are both outside of us and within us. The Second Step helps us connect with them all.

Every Day In Every Way

There is a wonderful Zen saying by Thich Nhat Hanh which says cleaning up after a meal can be curative to our spirits. However, our cleanup will only help us if we wash the dishes in order to wash the dishes, and not if we wash the dishes in order to get them done. The difference may seem trivial, but it is really tremendous.

When we wash the dishes to get them done, as most of us probably do, we abusively push ourselves to complete a disliked task. We rush to get through a few moments of living, and we will never be able to get those moments back. They and whatever potential they may have had are gone forever.

It's a completely different story when we wash the dishes in order to wash the dishes. Then we allow ourselves to value and even cherish the experience of warm water on our hands, the satisfaction of cleaning the plates and utensils and the lovely sense of non-pressing time. We actually have a healing experience washing the dishes. It may seem incredibly silly to describe dishwashing as a spiritual experience, but if we accept the wonderful possibilities offered by the task, it can be just that.

Our lives are full of spiritual resources that can help us heal. We feel connected with the entire universe as we stand and look at a starry sky on a winter night or watch the summer sun rise across the prairie. We get a sense of security from knowing there are other people, programs, books, leaders, medicines and activities that can help us learn and live better.

We get a feeling of confidence when we begin to believe in our own inner wisdom. We get comfort when we accept the healing energy of ordinary everyday living. As we eat, take a bath, meet with friends, make love, tend a flower, hold a child, watch a bird, write in a journal, meditate, stand up for ourselves in a difficult situation, feel the rain or the wind on our faces as we do any of these things, we can heal.

The Second Step helps us realize the spiritual potential that is all around us every day. Other people at other times have taught the same thing.

Zen teaches that the true realization of the life spirit occurs when we become one with whatever piece of life we are living.

Hopi Indians teach that everything is right here right now.

St. Catherine of Siena, a Christian mystic, said that all the way to Heaven is Heaven.

It is true that spirituality can't be separated from the common miracles of everyday life.

Restoration Of Innocence

We've come a long way from our original innocence. Once we were small, perfect people, open to life, trusting everyone and everything. Now we're not any of those things. Like everyone in the world, we've been damaged by the circumstances of our lives. Things happened to us, things hurt us. As grownups we don't have to take responsibility for the things that hurt us. They weren't our fault. But we do have to take responsibility for our restoration from them. We will never again be true innocents — the damage that has been done is a permanent part of our psyche — but the 12 Steps give us the power to reclaim our innocent openness and trust.

In *The Snow Leopard*, Peter Matthiessen tells us that as we work toward spiritual growth, *"The journey is hard, for the secret place where we have always been is overgrown with thorns and thickets of ideas, of fears and defenses, prejudices and repressions."* When we find our secret place and reclaim our innocence, openness and trust can triumph in our lives, and we can be restored.

What About Healing?

Then there's the question of healing. What is it that needs healing and how do we heal it? We have no open, draining wound that needs attention. It's our inner self that is sick, it's our inner self that needs help.

The Second Step means we can use the power of spiritual resources to heal ourselves. We can be cured of denial, chronic anxiety, depression, grandiosity, resentment and all the other negative states that wither our spirit. We can be restored to a place where our vision is clear and we feel competent, confident and trusting in our lives.

The healing of a self is a hard thing to live through. Many of the feelings that go with it seem negative. We have to use anger to clean our emotional wounds. We have to deal with fear as we try new ways to survive. We have to accept the confusion that protects us from feelings that are too harsh and change that is too rapid. So much of healing doesn't feel good.

And this is where the emotional and psychological energy of faith comes in. We simply have faith, we simply believe that if we continue the journey, things will get better. Our faith pays off and slowly our program works. We stick with it and it keeps on working.

There are times when it seems as though our lives are back where they were when we started, when we can't connect with any spiritual resources at all. Then there are times when we feel surrounded by calm and strength and beauty. Then there are the bad times again. Gradually the good times increase and the bad times get fewer and farther between. Our sense of self grows stronger. We have the feeling that inside of us is a core that feels calm and certain. We begin to heal. And from that healing place we begin to grow. We use our spiritual strength to begin to reach our human potential.

We Use The Power

"Came to believe that spiritual resources can provide power for our restoration and healing." If we do believe this, if we have

faith that spiritual resources are all around us and that they can provide us with power to heal and grow, how does that happen? It's different for each of us. Here are four examples of how it worked for four very different people.

Ann

Ann stands by a huge stormy lake. She is 65 years old, recently widowed, at a turning point in her life. The wind pounds at her body, the waves crash, the spray flies. Ann has come here because she needs to be alone. She needs to make a decision that may set a path for her new life. She tries to think, to balance the pros and cons of what she may do. But her mind swirls round and round, the same old thoughts over and over. So she tries to stop thinking, to simply watch the grandeur of the lake and the wind. She gives herself over to the rhythm of the moment she is in. Gradually her mind is cleared of its babble. Slowly she calms.

Then it happens. Her quiet mind releases a new idea, one she hasn't had before. From deep within herself has come an answer. And the lake and the wind have given her something, too. When she leaves this place, she will take with her an image, a memory, a feeling that she need never lose. When she feels alone, frightened, confused or weak, when she needs another answer to another problem, she can return to her memory of this time and use its energy. Always.

Tom

Tom is a 33-year-old father of two sons. He and his wife, Sue, are at the doctor's office. They were told three weeks ago that Sue had a terrible form of uterine cancer. She has had a hysterectomy and is just out of the hospital. They are meeting with the doctor for the final pathology report.

The doctor tells them the reports are good, there are cancer cells in only one lymph gland, Sue's disease hasn't spread as far as they feared. She will need radiation, which will be hard on her, but her chances for recovery are good. Tom's whole being soars with joy. This is the very best they could have hoped for. Tom stays centered in his joy, truly takes time to feel it, to root the explosion of happiness and wonder deep inside himself.

Tom knows there are going to be hard times to come. Sue will be sick from the radiation, the children will need special care, there may be a recurrence of the cancer. But the feeling of joy is a separate thing from whatever caused it. It is a source of spiritual strength. Tom knows that in times of future crisis or despair, he can reconnect with his joy and rest in it for a little while, girding himself to live with whatever struggle is on his path.

Sarah

Sarah is 24, recently graduated from business school and about to go on a special job interview. She is so nervous she can hardly function. She needs this job, she wants this job, she believes her professional future is at stake.

Sarah knows her nervousness could destroy the interview, yet no matter how hard she talks to herself, her jitters don't get any better. She stands tapping her perfectly-manicured fingernails on the window as she looks out at the potted geraniums on her apartment deck. They are a brilliant scarlet, glowing in the sunshine. A thought comes into her mind. She goes out onto the deck, breaks off a single geranium flower and takes it to the kitchen sink where she carefully wraps the stem in a wet paper towel. She picks up the flower when it's time to leave.

Sarah climbs into her car and carefully places the flower next to her on the seat. She drives off to the interview. In the company parking lot, just before opening the car door, she looks at the small vibrant piece of life lying next to her. It's still fresh and glowing and Sarah is comforted. She knows that no matter how the interview goes, no matter what turns her life takes, flowers will continue to bloom. And that's what's important. Despite anything that can happen to her, she will always be able to turn to this wonderful source of beauty and strength. She takes a deep breath and opens the door.

Jim

Jim is 44, a recovering alcoholic, a husband and father of three teenagers. He is competently fulfilling his career as a lawyer. Jim has just been told that his 16-year-old son has been caught dealing dope. He feels as though his world is falling in on him. He has worked so hard; worked at recovery, worked at fathering, worked at providing — and now this. His head spins. He feels out of control — where to turn?

Jim has been through treatment for his alcoholism; he knows the program and what the 12 Steps can do. He's seen it in others and experienced it for himself. So he goes to his study, closes the door and picks up one of his AA books. He reads quietly for an hour or so. As he reads the well-known words, his mind slows down and he begins to get a sense of perspective. He knows what to do about his son and what to do about himself. He also knows that this feeling won't last, but for this particular moment, he is peaceful.

Ann, Tom, Sarah and Jim are different people leading different lives, looking to different spiritual resources for strength. But what they experienced can happen for any of us. Each of our lives is played out against a backdrop of spiritual possibility, what the Hindus call "the beyond that is within." The possibility of spiritual energy available to us is endless. No matter who we are or what our problems may be, we can feel the power of the "beyond" if we believe and live the Second Step.

*Came to believe that
spiritual resources can provide power
for our restoration and healing.*

**Today I will believe I can
connect with spiritual resources that
will help me become the person
I want to be.**

CHAPTER FIVE

Step 3

Make a decision to be open to
spiritual energy as we take deliberate
action for change in our lives.

Principles: Decision, Acceptance, Action

· · · · · ·

Steps 1 and 2 call for reflection. They are the mental Steps of the program, calling for insight, honesty, faith and hope. Step 1 gives us insight into our faulty thinking and shows us the reality of our powerlessness. Step 2 provides a vision of hope for great positive change in our lives. And then there is Step 3, the Step that takes our recovery into the outside world. Step 3 calls for decision. Our decision is the bridge between the mental part of the program and the action part. The decision of the Third Step connects the possibility of change with the reality of doing it.

Activating Change

Having insight about ourselves and having hope that our lives can improve does not automatically produce change. Only change makes change. Change rarely happens by accident and good intentions don't do the job either. We must decide that things will be different and then follow through with action.

In Step 3 we activate our own winds of change. We decide, we open ourselves to spiritual energy and we commit ourselves to deliberate action. The interplay among these forces sets up a dynamic that soon begins to fuel itself and healing change becomes a true force in our lives.

What It Means To "Decide"

All living is a process of decision. Every waking moment of every single day we decide. We decide whether to get out of bed, what to wear, what to eat, who to talk to and what to say. Right at this instant you will decide whether to read another word of this book.

But we can't "decide" about everything. We couldn't get through the day if we had to "decide" to pick up a pencil or pull up a sock. These are habitual decisions that are grooved into our brain. They are only the background for the real decisions we have to make. Real decisions can be active and examined or passive and unexamined. Most of us guide our lives with unexamined decisions driven by our pain, our denial, our rage — in other words, driven by the roots of our compulsions.

The Third Step teaches us another way. We learn to make active, examined decisions. We push ahead in a time of crisis rather than fall back into our old ways. We learn to step back from ourselves, to take time and to apply new knowledge. With the help of the Third Step, we take full responsibility and begin to guide our own destiny.

Influencing Our Destiny Begins With Letting Go

In Step 3 we take charge of letting go. In order to physically let go, we have to consciously relax our muscles and allow the chattering in our minds to stop. We let go and the spiritual forces of peace, quiet and serenity bring about positive change in our bodies. We do the same sort of thing when we psychologically let go. We deliberately relax our mental grip on our belief in self-power. We let go of this delusion and are free to reach for new, positive energy that replenishes our spirit.

We Decide To Open

Some of us reject the very idea of spiritual energy. We fuss about whether it is good or bad or better or worse or whether it can be proved at all. It is only when we stop trying to evaluate it that we can reach for what helps us. We reach out, and if what we find opens a happier, more serene way, it is power we can use.

When we are open to spiritual energy, we have a serene relationship to life. We are receptive to what's around us — we notice things. We feel eager to learn from life and willing to live fully and happily. We begin to understand where we belong in the natural scheme of things. We adopt an attitude of appreciative openness, the attitude that some people call "living consciously."

We can open to spiritual energy with our emotions, our minds, the action of our bodies or with our whole being. We can draw inspiration from the natural world, from the power of ideas, from the courage of another person, from wisdom, from everyday events in our lives or from a larger purpose. There are many ways to make profound spiritual connections. Drawing from varied and changing sources of strength can give us a rich and fullbodied experience of feeling alive. We open to life, and life opens to us.

The energy for our healing comes from our letting go, from our openness, our reaching and our acceptance. In Step 2, Ann, Tom, Sarah and Jim each made a conscious decision to reach for their own spiritual energy as they faced change. What inspires us and how we experience it is personal. No matter what or how, the energy we gain is real.

We Commit Ourselves To Action

Step 3 is also a commitment to action, deliberate action springing from active decisions. Without action, the dynamic of change is inert theory. Without action, our decision is incomplete and is unconnected to the energy of healing. If we want to change, we must be willing to *do* change. Committing ourselves to action means we are willing to do hard things and feel hard feelings.

Change is very difficult. It's the very thing we have been steadfastly avoiding. Change takes patient, persistent practice in thinking, feeling and acting in new ways. But eventually, after we've worked at it long enough, we become what we practice — we learn to live well.

We Learn To Dance By Dancing

We each have our own life, our own truth, our own power, our own way of experiencing spiritual energy and moving through life. We will each arrange and activate the dynamics of change in our own way.

In *The Dancing Healers* Carl Hammerschlag says if we are to live in peace, we must connect with others and with something outside of ourselves. We can learn the universal, generic pattern of life's dance from the 12 Steps. But in our individual dance of life, we must choose our own music and dance our own dance. Our music must fit our needs and our own particular movements.

We have to consider many things when we choose our music: tempo, rhythm, volume, instruments, melodies and harmony. We must decide carefully. Our choice of music guides our dance and our dance creates our life.

We heal when we dance our own unique dance to our own unique music. All by ourselves we discover and practice our own personal movements. We can change our music and enlarge our form. We experiment and make mistakes. We experiment and succeed. Our dancing muscles get stronger. Our music and our movements become finely synchronized. It all works together and we love how it feels. We practice until we are dancing in a way that is exactly right for us.

Make a decision to be open to spiritual energy as we take deliberate action for change in our lives.

Today, at least once, I will reach out to a spiritual resource as I meet the challenges and opportunities in my life.

CHAPTER SIX

Step 4

---

*Search honestly and deeply
within ourselves to know the exact nature
of our actions, thoughts and emotions.*

Principles: Self-examination,
Personal honesty, Self-acceptance

• • • • • •

Step 4 helps us discover our true self and Step 5 teaches us to share it with other people. They work together to join us with the human race as who we are, rather than as who we pretend to be. Our life takes on a different reality as we change the way we know our own nature and the way we interact with other people. First, Step 4.

We want to change — we honestly want to change. We have tried and tried to make things different in our lives, but we haven't been able to find a way. Now we can let the Fourth Step help us. It tells us to search honestly and deeply within ourselves in order to know the exact nature of our actions, thoughts and emotions. We try to know and understand what we do and why we do it, what we think and why we think it, what we feel and why we feel it. Otherwise, there will be no change.

If you always do what you've always done, you'll always get what you've always got. If you want something different, you have to do *something different.*

Paul R. Scheele

We wouldn't be reaching for recovery if we didn't know that something was very wrong with our lives, if we didn't know that we needed to do something different. But we don't know what's wrong, and we don't know how to do anything differently.

Step 4 gives us a chance to do something new, to struggle with ourselves in a different way. As we work with this Step, we gain layer upon layer of deepening understanding about the things that make us tick. Some of those things we like and others we don't like at all. But at least once we acknowledge that what we find makes up our true nature, we have a realistic account of what needs to change and what strengths we have to work with. We discover who we have been, who we are now and who we have the potential of becoming.

I Know All Things, Save Myself

The first principle that underlies Step Four is self-examination. We examine what we actually do and the consequences of our actions. We examine what we actually think and the consequences of our thoughts. We examine what we actually feel and the price we pay for our feelings. But before we can examine all these things, we need to identify them. The job of *learning* who we are is the first and most essential step in *becoming* who we are.

To begin and to stick with a Fourth-Step search takes great courage and commitment. It is one of the greatest challenges of a lifetime and it's undoubtedly one of the hardest. Our fear makes it hard to carry a spotlight into the dark, dangerous corners of our mind. It's even hard to illuminate the strong, safe places, because we have learned that it's somehow perilous to feel strong or safe. It's hard because of the pain, it's hard because of the denial and it's hard because it seems never-ending. But practice makes it easier. We get better at it and more comfortable. Eventually the Fourth Step and the many different ways we learn to use it become the foundation of our psychological and emotional evolution.

What It Takes To Make The Search

Someone said that when we look outward, we see all our problems, small and large, littering the landscape. And also that when we look inward, we look to the source of them all. When we look inward, we find not only the source of our problems but the source of their solutions, too. But how do we go about searching ourselves deeply and honestly to know our exact nature and find the solutions to our problems? This takes certain skills of character, skills that will serve us well for the rest of our lives.

1. We Accept Reality Without Denial.

Our roadblock to knowing ourselves is denial. Denial means so many things. It means ignoring, rationalizing, justifying, pretending or refusing to consider the opinion of an objective observer when it isn't the same as our own.

Denial is when our husband has deeply hurt our feelings and we don't let him know, but we lash out at our child for spilling milk.

Denial is when we cruelly tease someone and then say it's "all in fun."

Denial is when we have a second piece of cake and tell ourselves we won't do it next time.

Denial is when we unquestioningly accept our son's explanation that the marijuana in his drawer belongs to a friend.

Denial is when we give a physically-abusive spouse a second or third or fourth chance.

We each have beautifully-crafted webs of denial about situations in our lives, about other people and, most deadly, about ourselves.

It's the denial about ourselves that the Fourth Step confronts. Each of us has a fixed, obstinate idea of who we are: what kind of personality we have, how we look, what our behavior is, what our motives are, how we relate to others and how others see us. For most of us this idea is based on past beliefs, on wishful thinking, on rationalizing and self-justification. In other words, our idea of who we are is based on denial.

A woman who was an overweight adolescent always pictures herself as fat, even though she has been a normal weight for the last 15 years. A wealthy executive refuses his family an expensive ski vacation because his own father was always out of work and there was never enough money. A notable scientist worries that he will never live up to the definitions of success he has set for himself. These people are all locked in denial, in self-delusion, in an unrealistic world. Their current reality is made up of rationalizations and justifications, not on the actuality of their lives today.

Others are locked in denial, too. There is the woman who always obeys the law, always follows society's rules and describes herself as absolutely honest. But she is unable to look at her dishonesty to herself. She is jealous of her younger brother's success and feels a throb of pleasure when he is not chosen for an important position, yet she smiles and tells people what fun it is to have a famous doctor in the family. She is never rude and never loses her temper, blaming the pain in her stomach on what she had for dinner. She cannot get past the initial lie that she is an honest person. Like so many of us, she believes that if she hides her true nature from others and hides it from herself, it doesn't exist.

And it *is possible* to hide our exact nature from ourselves and from society forever. All it does is kill our spirit.

It's hard to learn to see ourselves clearly, but self-examination is basic to a fulfilling life. If we are going to live the life we want to, we need to understand our real nature. We need to make considered and conscious choices instead of being driven by unconscious, reactive needs. Only then can we make realistic assessments of our current lives, no matter what our past has been. To search ourselves honestly and deeply helps us build the skill of seeing ourselves clearly, tearing away from our tenacious web of denial. We learn to set ourselves in the present and react to our current life according to our current self, not to a self that belongs in the past. The messages from the past no longer clamor for attention. We can rest in the quiet and open ourselves to spiritual energy from today.

2. We Discover Our True Motivations.

Another skill taught by the Fourth Step is to discover *why* we do what we do, *why* we think what we think, *why* we feel what we feel.

Why do we pick a fight with our husband when we know we've done something he disapproves of? Why do we resent the success of others? Why do we stay home and mope rather than make plans to be with a friend? Why do we refuse a job promotion that involves a lot of personal challenge? Why do we take on so many obligations that we can barely handle them? Why do we feed the stray dog that cries at our door?

As denial begins to clear, we find out all kinds of things about ourselves — and this can be exciting. Some of the things we find we don't like. We don't like finding resentments, righteousness, rage and fear. These things don't match the person we think we are. We don't like to think we deliberately cause fights rather than accept realistic criticism. We don't like to think of ourselves as jealous. We don't like to think we'd rather be alone because we still hurt from the rejections of childhood. We don't like to think we're afraid of a challenge because of old messages that tell us we'll never be good enough. We don't like to think we take on obligation after obligation so we gain a false persona while we lose ourselves under all that busy importance. But there are bright spots, too. We're glad we're the kind of person who takes on the responsibility of a homeless dog because he is a helpless creature who needs food and shelter.

The Fourth Step shows us we have motivations that are assets rather than liabilities. Our honest search uncovers love, compassion, determination, commitment and a sense of personal power. When we discover these strengths, we live differently. We choose to listen to criticisms from our husband without becoming defensive and lashing out. We realistically evaluate what he says and either change our behavior or decide his opinion doesn't match our own true needs. We're glad when a neighbor gets a raise and buys a gorgeous car. We meet freely with friends, take on new challenges and choose only the obligations that are compatible with ourselves. We find peace as we pet our dog.

3. We Accept Ourselves Without Judgment.

Denial begins to crumble. Honest motivations are found. Then what? How does our search go deeper? It goes deeper when we begin to work at examining ourselves without being ashamed of what we find.

Most of us can't remember a time when we weren't judged by others and didn't judge ourselves. We grew up with parents, grandparents, aunts, uncles, brothers, sisters, teachers and lots of others telling us when we were good and when we were bad. We came to accept their judgments. As grown-ups we still believe these old judgments, lecturing ourselves in much the same way our parents and all those other people lectured us in our formative years. We judge everything about ourselves — how we look, how we feel, how we act. Everything gets put on a continuum from good to bad. We lecture ourselves and judge ourselves and lecture ourselves and judge ourselves.

Self-acceptance without judgment is crucial to discovering the "exact nature" we are looking for. If we don't give up self-judgment, give up telling ourselves this feeling is "good" or that action was "bad," the Fourth Step — no matter how thoroughly or diligently we work with it — will be meaningless. We must accept objectively whatever the search into our true nature brings. This is the only way to come to peace with our true self.

Instead of self-judgment, our new rule becomes, "As I search my deep nature, anything I find is okay. It's not good, it's not bad, it just is." Objective searching and accepting doesn't mean we justify, excuse or condone any behavior that has caused others suffering or pain. We know there is no excuse to hurt anyone. But when we acknowledge our hurtful behavior, there's no point in mentally beating ourselves up either. Like all the "good" things we have done, the "bad" ones are simply a part of us — a part that is past. This kind of thinking allows room for a whole being to emerge.

Nothing "bad" has to be held down and buried by elaborate denial. Nothing "good" needs to be exaggerated or explained away. We simply are what we are. We have done what we have done. We think what we think. We feel what we feel. That's all.

Step 4 teaches us that accepting the negative things about ourselves leads to renewal. It's important to identify what we see as emotional liabilities so we can transform them. We stop judging ourselves with what's good or bad and start choosing our actions on the basis of what works or doesn't work. This means we choose to feel and act in ways that are useful to us and respectful of others.

───────■───────

SAM

Sam is 45 years old. He lives a quiet life, a life he has deliberately chosen for himself. He loves, is loved and makes enough money to support his family and put some aside for retirement. Sam likes the way he lives. Yet he has a constant, nagging feeling that he is not doing enough with his life; he is not as financially or professionally "successful" as he could be if he had been more aggressive and chosen a different way to live. He could still change, but he truly doesn't want to.

Sam is caught between his understanding of his true needs and an old judgment that he is somehow bad. He sees his unwillingness to pursue what society calls "success" as a weakness in his character. As he applies the Fourth Step to this situation in his life, he understands that his way of living works for him, is right for him and conforms to his true self. With this understanding comes peace.

One final thought about self-judgment: There is an interesting way that our reaction to other people can help us understand our own nature.

When we rage at someone else's hypocrisy, when we become upset at another's laziness, overindulgence or self-destructive acts, we'd better examine what we are really agitated about. Is our anger really directed toward another person or at our own hypocrisy, our own laziness, our own overindulgence, our own self-destructiveness? Are we really furious at someone else for acting out the negative traits in our own nature that we deny, hate, are afraid of or spend much time and emotional energy fighting against? Are we sending our anger outward because we don't want to send it inward?

These are all good questions to ask ourselves. The intensity of our outward response may be a measure of our internal judgment and an indicator of how violently we are abusing our inner self. No wonder it wants to hide.

4. We Realize Our Own Personal Strength.

Finding and accepting our true self takes honesty and lots and lots of courage. We are used to struggling and feeling weak and confused. Our personal strength is something we often discount. We try to control our world so we can feel strong, but just underneath the surface of our immediate consciousness lie feelings of fear and weakness. This is how we feel, but the reality is that we are very, very strong. If we weren't strong, we wouldn't be trying to heal. If we weren't strong, we wouldn't be trying to find peace and serenity in our lives. If we weren't strong, we wouldn't be looking for joy. Our commitment to the 12-Step program comes out of our strength. Our unceasing struggle comes out of our strength. Our growing sense of humility, of recognizing our place in the overall scheme of life, comes out of our strength. Our spiritual growth comes out of our strength. We always need to remember that *embracing our own strength is the key to our healing.*

We switch from thinking we are weak to knowing we are strong. Instead of accepting our feelings of weakness and struggle, fear and desperation, we can choose to acknowledge that we are strong. We can assume that we are operating from a core of strength and our strength is where our self lives. We set our feet firmly on the earth and stretch our body toward the sky.

All of this can be translated into personal power. Personal power comes from knowing when to stand strong and tall to hold up the weight of the world around us and when to yield, to fold into ourselves and let the world wash around us. When we know that yielding can be strong and isn't always a sign of weakness, we have a real choice. When we can truly choose to stand or truly choose to yield, we are people with personal power.

Each time we use Step 4 we practice self-trust, and over time self-trust grows and grows. We learn to trust our own search and trust where it leads us. We learn not to shy away from our own truths because *they* are who *we* are. We learn self-respect. We learn not to judge and abuse ourselves. In place of judgment and abuse we put love and understanding. We treat ourselves as dearly loved friends.

Everyone's Search Is Different

No one method of doing the Fourth Step is better than another. Each of us will discover many ways of examining our exact nature. Step 4 can be casual mental notes of self-revelation or it can be structured, formal and written. It can be written spontaneously in a journal or as carefully-thought-out responses to a systematic Fourth Step guide.

First-time Fourth Steps usually focus on problems in the present because persistent negative behavior must be arrested or slowed before we can go deeper into ourselves. Later Fourth Steps are more introspective, go deeper and often amaze us with what we find.

There are printed Fourth Step guides and inventories available, such as Carla Wills-Brandon's "The Fourth Step," (Health Communications, 1991). There are AA and Al-Anon conference-approved booklets and independently published guides. Fourth Step Weekends and Step retreats are offered in some metropolitan areas. We can use any or all of these sources of help, and we also learn to develop our own.

Our Search Evolves Over Time

The nature of our early Fourth Steps will be different from the ones we do later. In the beginning we usually work from the point of view of adults looking at our present lives. Our first Steps also tend to be formal. We make lists of our weaknesses, writing down every negative personal characteristic we can think of.

This kind of exercise is particularly helpful and important as a start. When we write down and address our negative traits, we unload painful thoughts, feelings and fears we work so hard to keep hidden from ourselves and other people. We begin the subtle and crucial process that introduces us to the injured child inside of us who is really running our show.

Later we begin to experience the Fourth Step through the eyes of our inner child or adolescent. This child carries our pain. Our adult self has spent immeasurable time and energy keeping this kid quiet. Acknowledgment of his or her pain, compassion for the carrier of so much agony, is the beginning of self-acceptance and self-love.

It isn't only our inner child that this Step shows us. The evolving Step gets us in touch with our childhood pain and also introduces us to our wise self.

Many of us have never considered that there is a wisdom that lives deep within us — but there is. While the hurt parts of us have lived out the pain, the wise part has also utilized our experiences quietly underneath the other. This part of ourself carries wisdom that we are unaware of, that our busy minds have been too frantic to discover. This wisdom is ours to use if only we will be still and listen. Recognizing both inner child and wise self, our character begins to balance.

We can narrow the scope of the Fourth Step and become much more specific in how we apply it. It can become informal and spontaneous, our natural way to approach a problem or challenge. Instead of looking at "resentment" as a general negative trait, we examine why we become resentful in a specific situation with a specific other. Instead of thinking about our "fear," we wonder why we feel uncomfortable around a certain relative. Instead of lecturing ourselves about overeating, we make detailed notes of what our feelings are when we want to go to the cookie jar. And we ask our inner child and our wise self to help. We finally acknowledge that they have a lot of our answers.

There is no "correct" way for this Step to evolve. We don't move directly from a formal Fourth Step directed by our current self to a deeper one led by our child or wise self. We bounce back and forth. One day we make a list of our troublesome traits, two days later we'll write down all our strengths and potentials. Another time we narrowly apply the Fourth Step to examine a childlike trait that shows up when we are criticized by a friend. Then we may ask our wise self to help. It's all useful. It all works.

Different Doorways To Step Four

There are many different ways to enter this Step, many different approaches to self-examination. Depending on which door we step through, we will cover distinctive landscapes and arrive at various destinations. Which door we choose doesn't matter, as long as we take personal honesty and self-acceptance with us.

1. Important events in our life, past or present. We choose an important event and examine our actions and reactions in relation to it. Perhaps we examine it through the eyes of our current self, our child and our wise self and note similarities and differences of these different approaches.

2. Personal attributes, assets and liabilities. We identify personal attributes as a way to learn about our exact nature. It's important to remember that most attributes have meaning only in the way we apply them. What we call "liabilities" may really be assets that are out of balance.

For example, self-control is an essential asset as long as it is used with moderation. It becomes a liability when we control ourselves in such a way that we are isolated, disconnected from friends or loved ones. Vulnerability is an asset when it allows us to express our feelings. It's a liability when we choose inappropriate times or places to be vulnerable so someone can use our vulnerability to hurt us. Step 4 can help us see both sides of an attribute and then consciously choose how to put it into action.

3. *Relationship between feelings and behavior.* We examine how our feelings relate to our behavior. Feelings and behaviors are *always* connected, sometimes appropriately, sometimes not. We look at anger, rage, shame and guilt and at what we do when we feel those feelings. Then we look at how our behavior affects both ourselves and others.

We can come at this from the opposite direction. When we yell at the dog, we can figure out what we are really feeling and toward whom. What do we feel when we act the way we act? How do we act when we feel the way we feel? The Fourth Step helps us to sort this out.

4. *Single behavior, large or small.* We identify a problem behavior and apply Step 4. When we first begin to use the Steps, we usually focus on something obvious such as drinking, gambling or allowing ourselves to be physically or emotionally abused. This is our initial concern. Later we focus on more hidden but equally hurtful behavior such as perfectionism, resentment or isolation.

One of the wonderful things about the Fourth Step is that it teaches us who we are underneath the major problems that brought us to the Steps in the first place.

5. *Single personal relationship.* We focus on a single personal relationship with our spouse, child, parent, sibling, friend or co-worker. We can look at this relationship overall or in terms of a single event. We examine our feelings about this person, how we relate to him or her, why we relate the way we do, what consequences we have to live with. We also examine whether we are actually relating to the person we are focusing on or whether that person is a stand-in for someone else. We try to sort all this out so we can see how much of it makes sense in our present life and how much is tied to the past.

6. Current situation. We examine a situation that's bothering us. First we carefully define what the situation is. Next we look at what we're feeling about it, what we're doing about it, how we're affected by it and how it affects others. Then we are in a position to decide how we can change it.

7. Balance of lifestyle. We look at the balance in our lives, at how we are juggling our work, social life, physical fitness program. We ask whether we are consciously caring for our mental and spiritual health. We may feel as though we're constantly teetering on a tightrope as we try to keep these things in order. We feel overwhelmed and lose the pleasure that work, family, friends or jogging used to give us. Step 4 helps us identify our true nature so we can decide what lifestyle balance best fits our unique needs.

8. Conscious versus unconscious messages. We ask whether the conscious messages we give ourselves are different from the ideas that appear in our dreams. There is often a wide disparity between the messages we get from our dreams, spontaneous images and "thoughts that come from nowhere" and the directives we give ourselves. If we are truly examining our exact nature, we'd better listen to the breakthroughs from our unconscious mind. These messages, whether we like them or not, are often gifts of honesty to be used to make deep change in our lives.

Reality Is Always Ours To Change

The Fourth Step is about changing reality. Everyone's reality is different. Two people can experience exactly the same situation and feel differently about it. They can even physically see it in contrasting ways. The world is made up of billions of people, each with a separate reality developing out of their particular set of genes and lifelong experience. And each reality is true for the person who lives it. Unfortunately, many of us live in a reality formed and limited by elaborate systems of denial. The Fourth Step helps us examine this.

An honest and deep understanding of ourselves is the basis of all our thought. This is important because it's our thought that directs the actions of our lives. It's true that the thoughts we think form our reality, whether that reality is honest or based in pretense and denial. As Henry Ford said, "*Whether you think you can, or whether you think you can't, you're right.*"

In every situation there are many ways to react. For example, if a friend forgets to meet us for lunch, we can be angry, understanding or laugh about it. We might be any of these. The important thing is that we make a thoughtful choice about what our response will be. Having the first reaction that comes is a primitive reaction that is often related to the pain of our childhood. If we follow through on our instinctive response, we are responding to a past reality. But Step 4 encourages us to change this. It helps us choose thoughts and actions that are appropriate — not to our past, but to our present.

The process is never smooth, and it doesn't ever seem to end. We will work this Step again and again. But when we get discouraged, we hang in there, we wait, we remember to breathe and pretty soon we begin to work again. It's hard and it's a struggle, but our healthy, hopeful, honest future is worth it.

Search honestly and deeply within ourselves to know the exact nature of our actions, thoughts and emotions.

Today I will closely examine the exact nature of one action, thought or feeling. I will accept without self-judgment whatever I find.

CHAPTER SEVEN

Step 5

---

*Will talk to another
person about
our exact nature.*

Principles: Trust, Personal Integrity

· · · · · ·

When we commit to the Fifth Step, we agree to "talk to another person about our exact nature." We agree to reveal to another human being the things we have found in our Fourth-Step search. This is not something most of us do easily. We would rather pick and choose among the things we tell others — we would rather carefully control the image we show the world. Step 5 requires that we change this. Talking with another person breaks down our emotional and psychological isolation, and we stop anxiously hiding our secrets. Working a Fifth Step is a safe way to allow our internal and external worlds to meet.

Most of us are afraid that if someone really knows who we are, they won't like us, they'll turn away. Step 5 teaches us this doesn't have to be true. Another human being can actually know all about us and still accept us. When our guide hears about our "bad" behavior and our "awful" thoughts and doesn't judge us, our shame lessens and its power fades. We no longer have to hide, protecting our secrets and problems. A guide's non-judgmental feedback helps us break through denial and decreases the probability of self-deception and helps us examine our values and explore new options. Finally we listen to our guides, really hear what they say and then have to confront our mental backtalk that instantly contradicts the good things others tell us about ourselves.

Our guides are important and we must choose them with care. A therapist, AA sponsor, spiritual advisor, physician — any of these will do. The only criteria are that the person . . .

1. Must have true objectivity (which rules out family, friends or anyone with whom we have or might have a social history)
2. Understand the Fifth Step, its purpose and his or her role in it
3. Be trustworthy
4. Know how to listen with non-judgmental respect.

Fifth Steps happen in many different ways. They can be emotional, mental or spiritual exercises. A Fifth Step can be liberating or seem to make little difference. It might have an immediate emotional or physical impact or have a delayed effect. The crucial thing about this Step is that we can do it and actually come out with our trust intact — we *can* trust ourself with another human being.

The way we do Fifth Steps will probably change as we become more comfortable with ourselves and with others. Early Fifth Steps are apt to be formal. We select a specific time to do the work with a chosen person. We may do this once or several times. As time passes and we become familiar with the process, we find that working this Step changes. It becomes increasingly informal and we do lots of "mini" Fifth Steps.

Our criteria for the people we choose as guides change, too. We may discuss a particular vulnerability with a spouse or trusted friend. We may tell a group of people about a particularly courageous thing we did. We never strip ourselves bare for the world to examine, but we discriminate, choose appropriate situations and talk. We have learned to identify with others and let them identify with us. With relief and joy, we have joined the human race.

Step 5 is a way station. It's a place to off-load painful memories that haunt and hurt, to leave behind things that hinder, hamper or slow our journey. It's a place to repack other things that will make our lives safer, richer, happier and more productive. It's a place to pick up a ticket to our potential. Our guide helps us be certain that, as we shake out and repack our helpful things, hurtful feelings and troublesome behaviors don't hide in the creases. We get back on the train and carry on with our journey, lighter and more free.

Will talk to another person
about our exact nature.

Today I will make an open and unpretending
connection with another person,
being faithful to myself in the process.

CHAPTER EIGHT

Step 6

*Be entirely ready to acknowledge
our abiding strength and
release our personal shortcomings.*

Principle: Willingness to change

· · · · · ·

Time and time again we've asked ourselves, "What's the matter with me? Don't I want to change? Don't I want to feel better?" And the answer is always the same: "Of *course* I do, of *course* I want my life to be better!" But someone standing on the outside watching our struggle would comment, "No you don't. You don't really want to change or else you would." In our heart of hearts we know this is true. We want to make our lives different but we don't know how — and we don't know what gets in our way.

Why We Don't Get Ready

Basically, we resist change because it's harder to change than to stay the same, even when staying the same hurts. There are powerful threats to becoming ready to give up the old ways and search out the new.

First, there is the fear of losing predictability and security — the fear of the unknown. It's a psychological truth that most people will stay in a bad place rather than change. They say, "At least I know where I am and what's going to happen." Even badly abused children will usually want to stay in an unsafe home, rather than move to a foster situation that's safe but unfamiliar. Whether we're adults or children, we're just too afraid to live with uncertainty or chart new territory.

A second threat to becoming "entirely ready" is our fear of facing what we have done, who we have been, who we are. To say, "I have hurt my daughter by controlling her, by not respecting her, by not letting her know how much I love her" is a very frightening thing. To let ourselves truly know our shortcomings and to experience the pain that goes with knowing them are always hard. But we have to acknowledge our past behaviors and ways of thinking and feeling if we are going to become entirely ready to release them.

Third, there is the fear that, if we *do* change, we won't know what to do with the person we become. What if we don't like him or her? What if we have to give up things we think are important? What if we do like what we find and then can't carry through over the long haul? We're afraid of giving up what we have without being sure of what we're getting. We're afraid of being stranded between the old and the new. Before we're willing to change, we want a guarantee that things will work out the way we want them to and that if they don't, we can go back to the old way.

And finally, there is the threat of the emptiness we are afraid of feeling if we release some of our pervasive shortcomings. We don't know what we can put in their place.

"I get a lot of energy from my anger. Where will my energy come from if I'm not mad at something?" "Sometimes I think I get bored when things go smoothly. I need a little chaos in my life." "What will happen to me if I don't keep busy all the time?" Anger, chaos and busywork are some of the negative feelings and actions that fill us up. We're afraid to let them go because we're afraid we can't fill the space they leave. This emptiness is something people don't often talk about or think about, but it is one of the major threats to becoming entirely ready.

How Do We Know When We're Ready?

A lot of books and experts tell us we have to "hit bottom" before we become truly ready to change our lives. Bottoming out is brought about by physical, mental or social suffering — or any combination thereof. And it's unique to each one of us. Hitting bottom doesn't always look like chaos. One person's life may look like a total mess and yet that person may be functioning very well. Another's may look in perfect order and the person may be suffering terribly. We can almost never tell when someone else hits bottom. But when *we're* there, our inner self knows it. That's when we reach out for help.

Not A Conscious Decision

Being entirely ready is not just a conscious mental decision. If we try to make our lives change by altering the thinking of our rational mind alone, it won't work. It won't work because becoming entirely ready has to happen in our subconscious thought, too. We must let go of our *subconscious* need to maintain a particular shortcoming or reject the idea of a particular strength. Being entirely ready happens only when our subconscious mind and our conscious mind get together and make the move.

• • • •

John quit smoking a dozen times. He read about the harm smoking caused, he went to a support group, he lectured himself, he did everything he knew how to do. Still he relapsed. Then one more time he threw away his cigarettes. He didn't smoke again.

Maria shopped. She didn't have the money to pay for what she bought, but she kept shopping anyway. She had terrible fights with her husband over her debts and then went shopping. She saw a therapist and cut up her credit cards. This helped a lot, and she began to do more constructive things than shop. One day she realized she didn't have any bills and didn't even *want* to buy anything.

Ruth never thought of herself as an artist. She said she was "a housewife, and sometimes I do a little sculpture." She discounted compliments on her work and shrank from praise. Her teacher encouraged her to have a showing; her friends encouraged her to sell through a gallery. Ruth practiced saying to herself, "I am an artist." She practiced saying "thank you" when someone said her work was lovely. One day she took a deep breath, called the gallery and asked to display her favorite piece.

• • • •

We will become ready when we are willing, accepting, open and calm. Somehow we know when "this is it," but we can't say why "it" happens. When we talk about being entirely ready, we're talking about a very mysterious process.

First of all, we *do* have to make an effort and we *do* have to be persistent in our commitment to changing behavior. There are many tools to help us. Some people join 12-Step groups. Listening to others and getting support is wonderful. Reading 12-Step literature offers insights. Keeping a journal can help. A knowledgeable therapist can help, too.

It's useful to go on spiritual retreats or to the woods, mountains, desert, ocean, our own backyard, wherever we feel in touch with the universal. We try to acquire good habits and practice them. We learn to quiet emotional self-abuse, to be firm but loving with ourselves. We continue to exercise our minds and learn.

We have to do what we can do to prepare, and then we have to let our subconscious and our spiritual strength take over. We have to let go. There are probably some people who can consciously "tough it out" and behave differently without subconsciously okaying the change. But they are like fish swimming upstream. Some of them make it, but the current is a problem all the way.

Conscious effort is only the first part of the solution, and by itself it won't change anything for long. Becoming ready is a two-level process. One is conscious effort, the second is yielding to the subconscious mystery. We do what we can consciously do, and at the same time we also think about yielding and being open to our own spiritual resources. We trust there is a deep mysterious process that finally allows us to change.

We Acknowledge Our Strength

At some level, conscious or unconscious, as we become entirely ready, we acknowledge that we have the strength to change. We've always said, "Oh, no! That's wrong! I'm not strong at all. I feel so weak and unsure." But the reality is that we are strong enough and secure enough to become willing to commit ourselves to turning our lives around. Otherwise we wouldn't do it. Whether or not we think so, the simple act of reaching for help comes from our strength. And not just from our strength, from our *abiding* strength.

Abiding strength is strength that lives in us and is *abiding* or continuous. Abiding strength is the basis of our natural, healthy spirit. It is beyond our conscious control and is always there to depend on. If we let it, our abiding strength will feed and energize our self-confidence and self-acceptance. Then our self-confidence and self-acceptance pour energy back into our abiding strength. This can become a wonderful continuous cycle that lasts a life-time.

Having abiding strength shows in many ways. A couple is strong when they sacrifice for their children's education. A working mother is strong when she goes home in the evening to care for her three children. A woman who remains calm and in control during her husband's cancer surgery is strong. So is a man who cries at his son's wedding. We see abiding strength when a person reaches inside, touches his or her self and does what that self suggests. In other words, abiding strength shows in personal integrity. And acknowledging this strength is one of the most healing things we can do.

We Release Our Personal Shortcomings

Our shortcomings are our thoughts, feelings and behaviors that hold us short of our full potential. They hold us short of our goal of a serene, peaceful, fulfilling life. They aren't bad, they aren't good — they simply exist as impediments to our growth. They hinder us. They need to be released and replaced with more useful ways of thinking, feeling and acting.

Most of us assume that releasing our shortcomings is the basic focus of Step 6. We examine our exact nature to find them, we mentally dissect them in a hundred ways and we try and try to get rid of them.

Because our lives need changing, it's natural to look to our shortcomings first and to try to get them out of our nature and out of our lives. But if shortcomings are the point from which we attack the Sixth Step, it isn't going to work. Of course we have to find our shortcomings. We have to recognize them and acknowledge that we need to release them. Then we need to put them on the back burner and get on with the real work of the Step.

The real work of Step 6 is to focus on our strength, examine what is in the way of getting ready and allow the mystery of our spirit to help. It isn't how much effort we put into releasing our shortcomings that makes this Step work, *it's our willingness to live without them.* We are entirely ready when we stop using shortcomings to quiet fear and anxiety, and instead we use our strength to accept our fright and to reach for spiritual help.

When we get into a situation where our shortcomings threaten to take control, we can say to ourselves, "Okay, how would a strong, comfortable person handle this?" Then we need to give ourselves time and room to be quiet and to listen. Not always, but most of the time, we will get some message or sign that tells us what to do. We may think the message is a great idea, we may not like what we hear or we may be afraid we can't do what the message tells us to do. Whatever our response is, we are ready for Step 7. Scientists tell us that energy is constant. It cannot be created or destroyed, only transformed. To be entirely ready is to take our energy and stand at the threshold of transformation.

Be entirely ready to acknowledge our
abiding strength and release
our personal shortcomings.

Today I will feel my abiding strength.
I will focus on one of my
shortcomings and consider the possibility
of living without it.

· CHAPTER NINE ·

Step 7

---

*Work honestly, humbly and courageously to develop
our assets and to release our personal shortcomings.*

Principles: Personal responsibility, Involvement
in change, Courage, Humility, Self-discipline

• • • • • •

We can't be a changed person unless we are
willing to make changes. Step 7 actually involves us in personal change. As we use this Step,
we go further than becoming willing to risk
change. We *do* risk and we *do* change. We risk, we
try, we fail, we start again. We act and our actions
change our lives. In Steps 4 and 5 we discover our
assets and our shortcomings. In Step 6 we become
psychologically prepared to deal with these qualities. Step 7 finds us ready to act.

Humility Comes First

When we become entirely ready to make changes, our abiding strength is stronger than our shortcomings. And humility is a crucial part of this spiritual readiness. We know we have learning to do and we undertake our lessons with humility and self-reverence. We measure our progress in relation to who *we* have been, instead of measuring ourselves against other people. We are taking our own journey. We acknowledge our strength and use it with humility, looking only for an honest way of living in an honest reality.

Then Work . . .

First we accept humility. Then we begin to work. So let's be sure we know what we mean by "work."

All of us can identify an action as work when it's deliberate or physically strenuous. Splitting wood is work. So is consciously gathering our courage to say no to the request of a friend when our guilts insist that we say yes. It may be harder to realize that we are doing important work when we let down old barriers and open our minds to new ways of thinking. It's work to allow ourselves to fail. It's work to stand up for ourselves. It's work to be patient. It's work to put up with the emotional discomfort of new ways. We can't judge something as work by whether it feels like work. We can't judge it by whether it results in the outcome we hope for. To work simply means to use our energy to be disciplined and committed in pursuit of our goal.

Effort And Action Bring New Freedom

We begin to change by actively letting go of our shortcomings, our actions and feelings that are liabilities. We cut our losses and start again. We begin by discarding old patterns of acting and old ways of thinking. We let go with slow, cautious and reluctant moves. No one lets go of shortcomings all at once. They disappear as we become aware of them, one at a time, over a period of years.

Our new rule becomes, "If it feels familiar, watch out. I'd better stop and look at this." When a friend hurts us, we stop before we try to comfort her and relieve her guilt. When our mother complains she hasn't heard from us for a week, we stop before we make a million excuses and try to make it right with her. When our wife is inconsiderate, we stop before we flare up and deliver the usual lecture. Whenever a reaction feels involuntary, it may be something that needs changing.

Change requires thought and planning. It also requires effort and action. Sometimes we work at changing a thought and then a changed behavior follows. Sometimes a thought just won't change, so we risk a new behavior anyway. Often, after we've used our new behavior long enough, changed thought will follow. We reinforce our new ways with practice, but mastery takes more than doing something over and over. It takes a high level of interest; it takes desire, thoughtfulness, commitment and constant vigilance. Step 7 requires us to be honest, courageous, humble and willing to do what it takes, even if it hurts.

Some of our shortcomings will stick with us despite our best efforts. Each of us is born with a genetic temperament. We can modify these traits but we can't lose them. Some of us have quick tempers. It takes others a long time to get angry. Some of us are inherently loners, while others would rather be in a crowd. Some of us are natural fighters, some natural lovers — it's just the way our genes work. Learning a healthy respect for the power of these traits is important, because then when they appear, we can collaborate with them instead of letting them take control.

As we let go of our shortcomings, we discover that we do not collapse. We expand. We are not left defenseless against life. Instead, we become less fragile, less explosive and less rigid. We gain breathing room. A wise person said, "Departure is the mother of hope." As we depart from our old ways, we have hope for a happier way to live.

We Exercise Our Freedom By Developing Our Assets And Making New Choices

Assets don't make us powerful over other people. Their only purpose is to empower us. We develop them by drawing on our inner strength. Assets are the things about us that make life richer, fuller and happier — things that give us a sense of well-being. They can be physical, mental or emotional qualities.

A high level of confidence is an asset. So is a special aptitude or talent. Attitudes and ideas can be assets, as are positive ways of behaving or an innate ability to get along with other people. Sensitivity to others is an asset, and so is an instinctive sense of self-survival. Assets can be deliberately learned or part of how nature made us. They may be hidden or obvious to everyone. Whatever form they take, each of us has a huge stock of them just waiting to be put into use.

We learn about real choice as we work Step 7. We finally comprehend that we have actual choices about how we act and think and feel. It's exciting to know we don't have to be the way we don't want to be. We develop our ability to see choice and to exercise choice. *We can actually change who we are by developing our assets, making new choices, and following through with action.*

The Downside Of Change

Change is risky. The 12-Step program doesn't guarantee specific outcomes to the changes we make. Some outcomes produce new problems. Self-respect and more independent behavior may make a spouse angry. When we stop trying to run our daughter's life, she may go wild for a while. When we refuse a friend's invitation to lunch, she may not call again. When we stop drinking in a favorite bar, we may spend many evenings alone. We always risk when we make changes, but with the tools we learn in the 12-Step program we can keep our perspective and deal with whatever happens.

Change is tricky. Step 7 has a predictable pitfall. At one time or another, every single one of us will think we are letting go of a particular shortcoming when in fact we are expressing it in a different guise. For instance, switching from beastly outbursts of rage to rageful, covert manipulation is not recovery. It isn't healthy just because we smile instead of scream. We must always stay aware of the power of our shortcomings to snag us. We are so practiced at self-deception that it sometimes takes even more pain before we understand our own games.

Change is slow. Deep and lasting change comes slowly, much more slowly than our impatient selves would like. Sometimes we have bursts of insight and rapid growth. We move along easily and are excited with our progress. We'd better enjoy these periods, because they certainly won't last. Most change is a matter of everyday practice, everyday recommitment day by day, thought by thought, action by action. We will probably spend the rest of our lives increasing our excellence in developing our assets and releasing our personal shortcomings. It's a grand way to live.

Assists For Working Step 7

Working the Seventh Step is like being in training. It lays out a lifestyle training regimen that builds inner spiritual strength and endurance. We make changes in the care of our body, the activity of our minds and the acceptance and expression of our emotions. We gradually bring the different parts of ourselves into a healthy balance as we practice new living skills.

In some cases our shortcomings will fade away as we practice. In others we need to make a conscious, deliberate effort to stop an old behavior and substitute another. The simple words "Stop," "Think" and "Start" can save us a lot of misery. When a feeling or an action feels automatic, we

Stop. Then we Think, which allows us to pull back and realistically look at the situation. Then exercising deliberate choice, we can either continue with what feels familiar or Start something else.

A common example is chronic worrying. Something happens and we start to worry about it. We worry and worry, even though we know we should be thinking about other things. So we Stop. Really Stop.

We make a conscious effort to step back, take time and Think about the situation. What good is the worrying doing? Is it going to make a difference in the outcome? Is it helpful to ourselves or someone else? Does it fulfill an emotional need? Then we Think about the answers to these questions and choose to either continue worrying or to Start doing something more interesting and productive. This sounds like a simple exercise. It's really very complex, but with practice it works.

There are lots of methods to help us learn new ways and practice them. Mental rehearsal or visualizing how we want to behave is one of the most powerful tools. Listening to people in a 12-Step group provides good ideas on handling similar situations in our own lives. Going to workshops and classes provides information that helps develop skills and assets. Reading can stimulate us and provide inspiration for change.

These are only a few of the ways that can be helpful — there are many others. By being open to trying new things, by purposefully experimenting, any of us can find methods that both work and fit our particular personality.

A final comment. We cannot force change in ourselves. We simply cannot do it. Forcing change is a fight against self and most often leaves us wounded, defeated and despairing. A lighter approach is *much* better. This is a mortal struggle, but it doesn't have to be deadly serious. Perspective, relaxation, a sense of humor, lots of love and forgiveness for ourselves — these are the qualities that are going to open the way. A useful slogan is, "Easy does it, but *do* it."

To Set The Goal . . .

In the past we have often set grandiose or inappropriate goals that condemned us to failure. It's important to set realistic goals we can actually attain. We are walking in a new way, perhaps in an altogether different direction and across unfamiliar terrain. We are likely to get lost or at least lose our footing now and then. When we are unsure, we take baby steps, keeping our goal in mind. We keep on going, but with caution. Every step, large or small, confident or hesitant, counts. And reinforcement is important. Again and again we tell ourselves, "Once is not enough," "Every time counts" and "Practice is what it takes."

Sometimes all of a sudden, after many tries, something we are working on clicks and we reach our goal. And sometimes we miss it by a wide margin. It's okay to fail because we learn from our mistakes as well as from our successes. And even though we miss our goal we're still on track, because we're moving in the right direction.

Effort alone is progress, and we value our progress more than we value the perfection of the outcome. We learn not to judge our efforts in the short term because deep and lasting change for the long term takes a long time.

Little by little, step by step, stage by stage, we will reach a goal. And when we look back, we can't really explain how we got there. So much depends on our willingness to "become entirely ready" and to work hard. So much depends on our willingness to be open to the spiritual energy that strengthens us. But for each of us it *will* happen, and we are grateful and we move forward.

*Work honestly, humbly and courageously
to develop our assets
and to release our personal shortcomings.*

*Today I will act on a plan to develop an
asset and release one liability.
I will remember that I can freely change
my plan as I move through my day.*

CHAPTER TEN

Steps 8 and 9

---

*List all people we have harmed, including ourselves,
and be willing to make amends to them all.
Be willing to forgive those who have harmed us.*

Principles: Compassion, Personal honesty and Accountability

*Whenever possible, we will carry out unconditional
amends to those we have hurt, including
ourselves, except when to do so would cause harm.*

Principles: Compassion, Change, Honesty
and Responsibility, Forgiveness, Self-discipline

· · · · · ·

Steps 8 and 9 go together, like 4 and 5 or 6 and 7.
With each of these pairs, first we look inward,
then we act outward. First we engage with ourselves, then we engage with the people around us.

- With 4 and 5 we discover our shortcomings, then share them with another person.
- With 6 and 7 we decide to accept our strengths and release our shortcomings, then work at doing this.
- With 8 and 9 we list those we have harmed, then make amends.

One of the reasons the entire program works so well is that it asks us to *think* and *act*. Neither one is enough alone — we need to do both.

When we start truly examining our harmful behavior, our load of guilt threatens to crush us. Guilt is relentless. It's the "gift that keeps on giving" — and giving and giving. In a subtle way it makes us feel better to feel guilty. Subconsciously we tell ourselves it's a bad thing to hurt someone else, so we should hurt, too. Our own suffering pays for our sins.

Instead of playing this guilt game, we need to take full responsibility for what we have done, make our amends and let the whole thing go.

With Step 8 we need to acknowledge that we've hurt others and are honestly willing to do something about it. We don't have to like making amends, we don't have to feel good about making them, we don't have to feel ready to do it. We just have to *do* it.

Being Sorry Isn't The Point

Being sorry and making apologies are not amends. Are we sorry we hurt someone? Or just sorry that they're mad at us? Are we sorry that we did something we shouldn't have? Or just sorry we got caught? How many times have we apologized for something, really felt as though we meant it — and then did the hurtful thing all over again and then again? How many times have we used apologies to manipulate others into giving us another chance?

Amends are different. *To make an amend means to change our attitudes and behaviors and to keep them changed.* Making an amend may mean apologizing, or it may mean making an internal commitment, but it *always* means changed attitudes and actions.

Amends are unconditional. We make them with no strings attached. We admit to another that we did a hurtful thing to him or her, we commit ourselves to not doing it again and we don't do it again. If we *do* do it again, our amend is worthless and we have to start over.

Amends are one-sided. They are valid no matter how the other person responds. He or she may accept our amend, criticize it or reject it. None of this makes any difference. We have examined our own selves, found our shortcomings and are making changes respectful of ourselves and others. This is the true meaning of making an amend.

Making amends means respecting others and it means respecting ourselves, too. If we put self-respect aside, our amends won't work. We mustn't grovel before the person we have harmed. We make the amend appropriate to the hurt, limit it to the hurtful situation and then get on with life. An amend is not meant to repair a relationship, only to acknowledge our mistake, clear our past and correct our future behavior. That's all. That's enough.

Pitfalls

There are always traps people can fall into while working Steps 8 and 9. Here are some suggestions that help us avoid them.

1. We don't have any expectations about what the other person's response will be.
   a. Don't expect forgiveness.
   b. Don't expect gratitude.
   c. Don't expect acceptance.
   d. Don't expect understanding.
   e. Don't expect reconciliation.
   f. Don't expect the other person to respond with an amend of their own.
2. We don't make the amend a tool of manipulation.
   a. Don't renege on the amend if we don't like the outcome.

    b. Don't make an amend to get someone off our back.

    c. Don't make an amend to buy time.

    d. Don't make an amend to get someone's praise or attention.

3. We don't look for a quick "feel better" fix.

4. We don't think our amend is the most important thing in the other person's life. It's easy to think we're more important to others than we are.

How To Do The Homework

Here are some guidelines that help us make amends. In using them it's important to be *precise and thorough*. We mustn't be vague. We mustn't slide over the hard parts. It helps to write them down. *Honesty is crucial.*

1. Person's name. Who did we hurt?

2. Memories of harm. What exactly do we remember about the situation?

3. Feelings about harm. How did we feel at the time? How do we feel about it now?

4. Thoughts about harm. What did we think at the time? What do we think about it now?

5. Motives behind harmful action. Why did we hurt the person we hurt?

6. What damage did we do? What were the consequences for the other person, for ourselves, and for the relationship?

7. Why do we want to make an amend? What are our motives for making it?

8. What specific new behavior are we going to commit ourselves to?

9. Exactly what are we going to do? Where are we going to do it? When is this going to happen?

10. Exactly what are we going to say? When are we going to say it?

11. What outcome do we want for ourselves?

Who Hurts Who And How

The harm for which we need to make amends falls into three categories: we hurt ourselves, we hurt others and others hurt us. We need to make amends in all these situations.

We Hurt Ourselves

The first amends we make must be to ourselves. Before we can make meaningful amends to others, we must acknowledge the hurt we have inflicted on ourselves during all the years we have been in pain. We cannot respect or love others before we respect or love ourselves. We cannot make true amends to others before we make true amends to ourselves.

The way we act with other people is a blueprint for the damage we do to ourselves. Treating others with disrespect shows disrespect for the person we want to be. Being dishonest with others can only mean we are dishonest with ourselves. Not letting others know our true feelings robs us of personal integrity. Denying we hurt others sickens our spirit. Denying that others hurt us is a form of self-abuse. And on and on. Steps 8 and 9 help us break this cycle of self-inflicted pain. When we make our first amend, we make it to ourselves. Under the first guideline, "person's name," we write our own. We commit our future to self-respect. We put our future in the hands of our strong self.

We Hurt Others

We have a list of people we have hurt — probably a very long list. Perhaps a list that seems overwhelming. But we don't panic, we just begin to sort it out. We're objective and refuse to let overpowering guilt get in the way.

We say, "I have hurt: . . . husband, wife, children, brothers, sisters, mother, father, other relatives, friends, acquaintances, institutions, myself (not to mention dogs, cats and other animals)." We take these one at a time and take months, even years, to deal with them. We make some amends and take time out to breathe. Then we make more amends. We're in no hurry. There's no deadline.

When we think about it, there are innumerable ways to hurt others. Harm can be physical or emotional. It can bruise the body, mind or spirit. It can be caused by things we do or things we neglect to do. Here are some ways we hurt other people, *not* in order of importance or degree of damage.

Overprotection	Lying, dishonesty
Neglect	Demanding
Rejection	Lazy, not doing share
Putting others at risk	Sabotaging
Setting bad examples	Negative comparisons
Unaffectionate, cold	Denying other's reality
Careless driving	Indifference
Unfaithfulness	Intolerance
Stealing	Disrespect
Laughing at, disregarding	Demanding
Criticizing	Verbal abuse
Pretending to listen	Threatening
Pretending to care	Yelling
Callousness	Evasion
Refusal to listen	Controlling
Judging	Gossiping
Overinvolvement	Grouchiness
Power plays	Tardiness
Withholding	Teasing
Hitting, slapping	

We tend to focus on the big hurts and forget that little injury after little injury grows into big damage. Amends are tricky because harm can come from positive as well as negative behavior. When we wrap someone in concern and care "for his own good," we may have the very best of intentions — but the person is smothered. If we are constantly cheerful and keeping others happy, we don't allow them to express their fear, depression or anger. We have to remember that we are people who have been hurt and we'll probably pass that hurt on in one form or another.

Sometimes if we are confused about whether we have hurt someone, it is appropriate to ask him or her about it.

We don't have to agree that what we did was harmful, we just have to accept the other's reality.

If a person feels hurt, harm did occur. People can usually tell us the extent and nature of what we have done and what they have suffered from it. We're lucky if they will do this. It cuts through everyone's denial and builds trust.

People Hurt Us

Most of the time it's fairly easy to recognize when someone injures us. They do something and in response we feel hurt, angry or afraid. But then there are the times when we feel hurt, angry or afraid and can't figure out what it was the other person did. Some people seem to smell our vulnerability and harm us in small, subtle ways that we can't explain. Some people know us so well they can easily zero in on our softest of soft spots. We ask ourselves who makes us uneasy, who makes us angry, who confuses us, who do we resent or want to avoid? Usually these feelings are clues that we are being harmed, and we need to listen to them. It's often hard to hear our feelings speak because we don't want to hear what they tell us. We want the other person to care for us, not hurt us. But in many cases, it isn't going to work out this way.

When we are hurt by others, we don't make amends to them, we make amends to ourselves. This means we change the attitudes and behaviors we direct toward ourselves, and the best amend we can make is self-respect. We need to alter or sever relationships with abusive people. We need to stand up for ourselves and understand that our best protection is to learn to be assertive. Our first commitment must be to treat ourselves with respect, the same way we strive to treat others.

To Err Is Human . . . To Forgive Is Hard

Step 8 tells us we must be willing to forgive others for the pain they have caused us. As long as we don't forgive, we hold onto our injury until justice is done. It's a consuming job to make sure people pay for the hurt we feel.

It's poor use of our emotional energy and it constricts our spirit. It also keeps us negatively attached to the person who hurt us.

When we forgive, we're not freeing the other, we're freeing ourselves.

It's hard to render continuous justice, but it's hard to forgive, too. We have to be entirely ready in order to forgive, and a lot of fear stands in our way.

In the first place, we're afraid to forgive because we're afraid we'll "lose." We're afraid we'll become defenseless or some kind of doormat.

This isn't true. It isn't true because we couple forgiving with self-respect. We forgive the other and respectfully promise ourselves that we won't allow that kind of hurt to happen again. We mean it. And eventually, after lots of practice, it doesn't.

Second, we're afraid that if we forgive, we're condoning the hurtful thing someone did. This isn't true either. Forgiveness isn't approving of, it isn't saying, "That's okay." It's letting go.

Forgiveness is neutral detachment. Forgiveness is letting go, without anger or anxiety and with much self-respect, the feelings that went with the hurtful incident.

"Forgive and forget" doesn't often work. We may never forget what happened, but we can learn to forgive, to let go of, to detach from the pain that went with it.

Forgiveness, neutral detachment, is not for the other. Forgiveness is for us. And forgiveness is not a way to stay attached. When we forgive, we may or may not repair the relationship with the person who hurt us. Our relationship with that person is not the issue — our emotional relationship with the hurtful situation is. Forgiveness sets us free from that relationship and consequently from our hurt.

It seems that practicing forgiveness is closely tied to Step 6. For example, let's take resentment.

Resentment is a base-line shortcoming, it's common and it's deadly to emotional health. Most of us suffer from carrying much too much of it. We resent our husband or wife for past hurts, we resent our mother for not caring for us in the way we wanted her to, we resent our friend for seeming distracted when we need help. When we practice forgiving these people, when we become neutrally detached from the hurts they have inflicted on us, we get closer and closer to being free from resentment. Then we can use that energy for something that expands our spirit rather than shrinks it.

Forgiving is a long-term process. We have accumulated lots of hurts over the years and now we forgive them.

The first person we forgive is ourselves. We forgive ourselves for allowing others to hurt us. We detach from the self-judgment that tells us we were bad, dumb or weak to be in a harmful situation. We forgive ourselves for denying our true reality and rejecting our true selves. We also forgive ourselves for hurting others. After we have started to forgive ourselves, we remember and forgive others who have hurt us. We let go of the guilt, shame and anxiety our memories bring back. Forgiving is a way to energize our spirit. We are strong enough to do it.

*"We Will Not Regret The Past, Or Wish To Shut The Door On It."

Steps 8 and 9 help us cut, strand by strand, the painful emotions that bind us to our past. They give us a chance to remake our present by changing our response to the things we have done to others and others have done to us. Our past loses its power. We gain an increasing sense of personal power and emotional freedom. We don't have to use our precious energy to bury or rationalize things we have done. We learn how to protect ourselves and have a better sense of how we shape our own lives. We let past mistakes teach us how to live in the present. We release our hidden hostility, resentment, jealousy and anger so we are not apt to pass them on.

---

* AA Big Book, page 83.

Making amends teaches us humility, and we are surprised that it feels more comfortable to be humble than grandiose.

When we make amends and practice forgiving, our relationships with the people involved will change. Whether we express our amends with words or simply carry them out with actions, people will react to our new ways. Some people may not really care about us or our amends. Others may actually trust us again. Some may not even notice, and we needn't point it out. Some will say, "It's about time" or be hostile and berate us. Still others will resent our amends and want us to go back to our old ways.

Whatever happens, the other person's reaction is no excuse to change our amend. No matter what the response of others, we are responsible for what we do. We choose to amend our past and be willing to forgive.

List all people we have harmed, including ourselves, and be willing to make amends to them all. Be willing to forgive those who have harmed us.

Whenever possible, we will carry out unconditional amends to those we have hurt, including ourselves, except when to do so would cause harm.

Today I will practice an amend. I will also practice forgiving someone who has hurt me.

CHAPTER ELEVEN

Step 10

*Continue to monitor ourselves, to
acknowledge our successes
and quickly correct our lapses and errors.*

Principles: Perseverance, Integrity

• • • • • •

Step 10 moves us into the maintenance Steps of
the program. With it we practice the unfailing
discipline of regular self-examination, and we
monitor the everyday workings of our lives. Consistently working the Tenth Step is an ongoing
commitment to ourselves and our program. We
demonstrate perseverance as we continually practice the skills of accurate self-appraisal. Then we
demonstrate integrity as we follow through and
correct our errors.

Step 10 is a practical approach to self-examination, and it's a gentle one as well. Our self-correction needs to be loving and firm. We mustn't attack ourselves with the weapons of self-blame and reproach. We monitor and correct ourselves for our own good, kindly, with great care, the same way we would correct a child we love.

Errors And Lapses Are Normal

There will be many, many times we make mistakes and fall back into old ways of thinking, feeling and behaving. This is to be expected. Spotting an error and stopping that particular thought, emotion or action seldom means we're through with it. Old ways die hard. We all have troublesome behaviors, thoughts or feelings that we've stopped dozens of times. Stopping is the easy part. Staying stopped is what's hard. Staying stopped means we have to monitor ourselves every single day. And we have to persevere.

We lapse in lots of different ways. We make the same old mistakes and we think up new ones. But we learn from all of them, we correct ourselves and the process goes on. We gain perspective. We learn to ask, "How am I going to feel about this a year from now?" And we learn to encourage ourselves with humor. We laugh with ourselves as we stumble in the same place for the tenth time, and we gently remind ourselves to lighten up and try again.

What Do We Monitor?

We monitor our moods.

A mood is a general emotional umbrella that can cover lots of different individual emotions. Part of Step 10 is to watch out for moods that get in the way of our progress. The list is long — boredom, unusual fatigue, the kind of stress that enervates rather than the kind that invigorates, anxiety, depression, hyperactivity, any of these moods can set us back. The purpose of Step 10 is to catch them early, before they have a strong hold on us. Then we can use what the Steps are teaching us and quickly correct them.

We monitor our emotions.

We must be on the lookout for all kinds of negative emotions. The principal ones to watch for are fear, anger and resentment. These emotions often lie hidden behind our motives and behaviors and are terrific at undermining our very best efforts to change. We can monitor fear and anger by first learning how these emotions feel in our bodies. Stomach tense? Jaw clenched? Face feel hot? Hands feel cold? Sweating? Shivering?

Body clues almost always tell us when we are angry or afraid, even when our head tells us otherwise.

When we monitor our body feelings and trust them, we can start to think about why we might be upset. Knowing the reason helps us decide what actions to take. We may see that our fear is well-founded and that we are afraid for good reason. This helps. We may see that our fear is only in our heads and can be overcome by doing what we fear. This helps, too. When we know why we are angry, we can make decisions about how best to deal with it, what to do about ourselves and how to deal with the situation that triggers our anger.

Then there is resentment. Resentment is an anger that we hold close to our hearts. We stroke it, we love it, it's our great justifier. Resentment is the secret weapon we use to inflict mental justice on somebody else. It acts as our shield and our protector.

The problem is that resentment always backfires and injures us, while the other person stays blissfully out of harm's way. Resentment eats at us, limits us, keeps us attached to the person we resent, steals our precious emotional energy and wastes our precious time in dreams of retribution and retaliation. And resentment is like a bad virus. Just when we think we are free of it, we find ourselves sick again. It's hard to let resentment go.

Usually resentment is the result of not forgiving, so the way to deal with it is to make a conscious effort to forgive. We deliberately practice detachment, an attitude of objective neutrality toward the resented person. We don't wish them ill, we don't wish them well, we cultivate objective neutrality. We think about the Eighth Step and all we learned about forgiveness.

Finally, after lots of conscious practice, lots of deliberate detaching, we can come to the point that what happens to the other person is no longer our concern.

We monitor our thoughts.

There are all kinds of thoughts that get us into trouble — so there are all kinds of thoughts we need to monitor. Here are some to watch for:

Obsessive thought. Is there something we just can't seem to stop thinking about? No matter how we tell ourselves to stop, do we keep going back to it? Do we think about it during the day and when we wake up at night?

Recycling thought. Do we mentally recycle the past, replaying the same scenes or the same emotions over again and again in our mind? Do the thoughts seem to run in circles, like a hamster in a cage?

Denial. Do we get into patterns of rationalization or self-justification? Do we persist in beliefs even though they don't match objective reality? Do we hang onto old ways of behaving just because it's more comfortable to do that than to change?

Negative thought. Do we leap to the negative conclusion instead of looking at the positive possibilities in a situation? Do we forget to ask ourselves (and really mean it), "What can I learn from this?" Do we forget that there is power in a peaceful frame of mind and that peace is impossible when we think negatively?

Overinvolvement. Do our thoughts revolve around a particular person? Do we plan and think and ruminate about how we are going to "make things better" for him or her? Do we just *know* we have the answers that will help?

We monitor all these kinds of thoughts — and we ask ourselves these kinds of questions about them. When some of the answers are yes, we do something to change.

We Monitor Our Relationships.

The way we get along with others is usually a good indicator of our well-being. We need to continuously monitor all the relationships in our lives. Regular upsets in our relationships are a sign that we need some correction. We examine our marriage/love relationship, the relationships with our children, other relatives, colleagues, neighbors, co-workers and friends. These are some of the areas we look at:

Respect	Trust	Caring
Compassion	Time spent	Play
Sexuality	Reciprocity	Cordiality
Intimacy	Fulfillment	Detachment

Monitoring all our relationships all of the time seems like a huge job — overwhelming perhaps. But we start out slowly, and before too long, this kind of monitoring becomes the natural way we approach a relationship. Sometimes we find the problem lies with us and sometimes with the other. Most often both people contribute. We need to correct our part and only our part. We may need to change ourselves within the relationship, we may need to build more distance into it or, in some cases, the correction requires leaving.

We monitor our work.

Everybody works. Work is what we do. It may or may not be connected to employment and has nothing to do with money. Bank presidents work, housewives work, hermits work — the question is whether whatever we do is rewarding and fulfills us. Are we content with our work? Are we interested? Do we do our best? Would we like to do something else? What we do and how we do it matters to our sense of well-being and self-worth — it matters a lot. If our work doesn't reward us or make us feel good about who we are, we need to take corrective measures.

We monitor our finances.

How we handle money is an important indicator of our inner state. Do we live within our means? How many credit cards do we use? Do we overspend with them? Is money a problem in our relationships? Do we overestimate our financial resources? These are questions for overspenders.

Then there are the others who can't seem to spend money no matter how much excess they have. Do we feel we "just can't spend that much on a dress," even though we really need or want it and have plenty of discretionary income? Do we always put off that wonderful vacation until next year "when we have a little more money"? Are we realistic in planning for the future? Do we spend beyond ourselves or beneath ourselves?

Whether we overspend or underspend, monitoring the way we handle our finances can be a very helpful clue to potential problems. An objective moderate approach to financial management is our goal, and correcting our "lapses and errors" is the way to get there.

We monitor orderliness.

Orderliness may seem like an odd thing to be concerned with. But, like finances, it gives lots of cues about our mental condition.

On one hand, we can look for signs of disorganization in our lives. Are we often late? Is our car a mess? Are our shoes scuffed up? Do we mislay things, lose things? Do we run out of clean clothes or groceries or dishes? For many people, a messy environment is a sign of inner confusion.

On the other hand, there are those who are more orderly than necessary. *Never* are they late. *Never* does their car need cleaning out or their shoes need shining. *Never* is a bed unmade or a dish left in the sink. *Never* do they run out of clean socks. For these people, over-orderliness is often a clue to a compulsive need to control.

We monitor our physical condition.

We can't realistically expect to grow spiritually if we abuse our bodies. We need to monitor the food we put into them and the exercise and rest we give them. We need to be careful not to overdo or underdo any of this. It's harmful to be a couch potato, and it's harmful to be an exercise addict. It's unhealthy to exist on bacon cheeseburgers and it's unhealthy to live only on brown rice. We must monitor ourselves so we can correct our mistakes when we make them and live with the physical moderation that is truly healthy.

We monitor our boundaries.

In a sense, personal boundaries are what the 12-Step program is about. We need to learn where we stop physically, mentally and emotionally, and where another person starts. We need to know how to live within our own skin and how to *stay* there. The Tenth Step requires ongoing monitoring of our boundaries so when we step outside of them, we can correct ourselves.

Do we give unsolicited advice? Do we think we have the answers for someone else? Do we physically touch people without permission, hugging them, touching their hand or brushing lint off their jacket? Do we stand too close? Do we interrupt when someone else is talking? Do we recognize when someone else has overstepped their boundaries? Do we know how to keep them from taking advantage of us? Have we learned to say no and stop? Step 10 helps us to be vigilant — to watch our boundaries and the boundaries of others.

We monitor the balance in our lives.

Finally we monitor both the mental and physical balance in our lives. Balance is one of the hardest things for most of us to come to — and it's crucial for a healthy life. Balancing our physical life is probably easier. We can look objectively at the ratio of time among work, relaxation and exercise and make adjustments. Mental balance is more difficult.

In order to find balance in our inner lives we have to attend to all of the things we've been talking about — our emotions, thoughts, moods, relationships, work, finances, orderliness, physical condition and boundaries. When we monitor ourselves in all these areas, correct ourselves and find self-respect and moderation, we also find inner balance.

It's helpful to know that inner balance is probably not a permanent state for anyone. There are just too many influences, both internal and external, that keep tipping the scale. We practice monitoring and with time we develop an automatic sensor that signals us when something about ourselves is off. We learn what it feels like to be "off" in our body or "off" in our emotions and thoughts. We may not be able to put our finger on it, but we know things are not right, and we instinctively know how to make the correction. We bring ourselves back into balance until the next time.

Different Ways Of Monitoring

It helps to have a ritual we regularly follow when we work with Step 10. We may do our monitoring every morning before we get out of bed. Or our ritual may be sitting down with coffee in the late afternoon and checking our day's progress. We may ritually write in a journal after we get into our pajamas at night. Or we may have a set time to speak with our sponsor. Rituals help us make a habit out of monitoring. Here are some techniques we can use.

1. We can do a quick spot check at any time. We may be caught in a traffic jam at five in the afternoon. We check out our feelings and correct our impatience and anger. We check out our thoughts and correct our assumption that we'll be late for dinner and our friends will be furious. We stop drumming our fingers on the steering wheel, take a deep breath and deliberately relax our tense muscles. We practice Step 10, and it helps.

Spot checks are a good time to use ritual language. When we monitor ourselves and know we are "off," we can say HALT to check whether we are Hungry, Angry, Lonely or Tired. We can say Keep It Simple, Easy Does It or Live And Let Live. We can say Progress, Not Perfection. We can remind ourselves to Take It Easy, or live One Day At A Time. We can say the Affirmation of Serenity whenever we need to, whenever we want to.

2. A daily review is a more leisurely type of monitoring. We do it early in the morning, during a lunch break, in the evening, whenever we have a few minutes for deeper reflection. We think about how we have worked with the Steps during the last 24 hours, where we've succeeded and how we might want to change. We think about the next 24 and might rehearse our corrections or think through a specific plan.

3. A daily "I will do" check list is very helpful to stay in touch with Step Ten. This is an example; we can all make up our own.

Today I will . . .
Do something for someone else
Do something for myself
Do something I don't want to do that needs doing
Do some physical exercise
Do something that takes real thinking
Take time for reflection and gratitude

4. Another technique is to write in a journal or diary — a journal or diary no one else will ever see. We put down our feelings, actions, motives, thoughts, ideas, seeds of ideas, inspiration, thanks. We can draw. We can write poetry. Whatever we put in our journal, we can review as a way to greater self-understanding. This kind of personal record is also a wonderful monitoring tool — it can make us feel great about the progress we have made or bring us up short when we realize we've been running in a circle.

5. Finally, several times a week we can check in with a trusted person who understands how the 12 Steps work. This person can be a sponsor, a good friend or a relative we are sure has our best interests at heart. He or she can guide us while we look for progress and examine problems that need correction. This method often leads to our being able to check with ourselves — we come to understand so well what the other person will say that we hear his or her voice in our heads.

The AA 12 x 12 book tells us that successful self-monitoring calls for self-restraint, honest analysis, willingness to admit fault and willingness to forgive when fault is elsewhere. It's hard, but we can do it.

Continue to monitor ourselves,
to acknowledge our successes
and quickly correct our lapses and errors.

Today I will carry out a plan for monitoring
myself. I will acknowledge my successes
with as much enthusiasm as I notice
and correct my lapses.

CHAPTER TWELVE

Step 11

---

*Increasingly engage spiritual energy and
awareness to continue to grow in abiding strength
and wisdom and in the enjoyment of life.*

Principles: Openness, Connection to life
and Spiritual resources

• • • • • •

Step 11 carries the spiritual concepts of Steps 2
and 3 into our daily lives. Our spirit is our life
force, and our spirituality is expressed in the way
we relate to the world through our thoughts, attitudes and actions. Everyone is spiritual. The question to ask ourselves is whether we are moving
with positive spirituality or whether our spiritual
energy is taking us in a negative direction. Positive
spirituality nourishes life, negative spirituality dim-
inishes us.

The text in Step 2 tells us that positive spirituality comes from whatever gives us hope, strength and peace and enhances our humanity. We learn to recognize, accept and engage the resources that help our spirit grow. Step 11 encourages us to engage spiritual energy and awareness to . . .

1. Grow in abiding strength
2. Grow in inner wisdom
3. Grow in the enjoyment of life.

Spiritual Awareness Is Self-Awareness

Spiritual awareness is an intensely individual thing. What is spiritually helpful to one person may be meaningless to another. Having full awareness of what gives us hope, strength or peace does not mean we can analyze spiritual energy. We can't know what gives hope, strength or peace to others, either. Our only responsibility is to recognize and use what helps us.

Spirituality is engaged most completely by fully developed and fully defined people. When we worked on Step 4, many of us admitted we didn't really know who we were or where we were going in life. In our culture each of us is socialized into a diminished life.

Men are programmed to show an aggressive, puffed-up personality that keeps them from knowing the soft, vulnerable parts of their nature.

Women, on the other hand, are trained to appear passive and receptive, which ensures that they won't know they can be confident and assertive.

If we accept our social programming, we become adults without truly defining ourselves and without being intimately acquainted with our strengths and weaknesses. This lack of definition constricts our spiritual potential.

People who have a strong, thorough understanding of their true nature are more engaged with life and as a result are aware of more ways to engage spiritual energy. So if our goal is to have a life filled with positive spirituality, we must dedicate ourselves to our own personal development.

Ways To Engage Spiritual Energy

When we engage spiritual energy, we don't turn our minds off. We keep our full capacity to think and reason. We decide what fits for us and we reject the rest. We are still reasonable human beings, and in addition we gain access to a treasure that runs along a different vein. We can tap into this treasure any time. We live with increasing sensitivity to ourselves and everything around us.

The world is full of spiritual resources, from the energy of the universe to the simple joy we feel when we receive a small gift from someone we care about. Here are some of the many ways we can engage it.

We Live In The Present

Spiritual energy is available only in the present, only in our Here and Now. We engage it by paying full, conscious attention to the moment we are living. We deliberately put aside thoughts about the past and anticipation of the future.

When we are tired, harried and rushing to finish our errands, we consciously engage with the here and now, rather than worrying about all the things we have left to do. We smile and chat with the counter person at the dry cleaners; we take a moment to appreciate the sharp sweet smell of fresh pineapple at the market.

We find moments of peace and pleasure. When we are lonely or depressed, we carefully watch the squirrels chasing each other around an oak tree or find a book that will absorb us or music that will lift our spirits. We find a little hope, strength or inspiration. It's the present moment we have a choice about — this instant we can choose energy that enhances us.

Wonder and curiosity happen only in the present. The spiritual energy of curiosity and wonder moves us toward new experiences. It leads us to try new things. We explore what catches our fancy. We experiment. We do old things in new ways and are openly curious about the outcome. Wonder and curiosity help us shed our biases and rigidity so our childlike creativity, optimism and acceptance are available to us — so we can engage with the spiritual energy of Now.

We Accept And Take Care Of Ourselves

Our spirituality extends as far as our self-acceptance and well-being. Positive spiritual energy is not available to men and women who reject themselves.

We could call the 12 Steps a selfish program — but it's really just a self-caring way of living. This means our first and most basic commitment is to ourselves. We are responsible for our own lives; no one else is going to take care of us. And "taking care" means not neglecting any part of ourselves. Good food and exercise take care of our body, self-respect and mental stimulation take care of our mind, insight and self-acceptance take care of our emotions. This kind of lifestyle means we are always moving in a positive direction and, once we are on the lookout for it, we will find lots of spiritual energy along the way.

We Look For Joy

We look for the positive. We ask ourselves what's useful in every situation. Even when we are faced with things that are unpleasant, painful or frightening, we can find positive ways to grow. This isn't denial, it's just learning an optimistic attitude toward life. This isn't being a Pollyanna, it's just being practical. There is a huge difference between a mind set that moans, "Woe is me — catastrophe, catastrophe," and one that says, "Okay, so this is what's happening. Now what can I do about it?"

Life is full of ever-increasing possibilities if we broaden our outlook so we see mental, physical and emotional options. By seeing the glass as half full rather than half empty, we see abundance and solutions, not deficiency and problems. We grow closer to being the kind of person

Sara Teasdale calls, *"One who makes the most of all that comes and the least of all that goes."* Joy becomes a dependable companion and a great source of strength.

We Have Activities And Hobbies

We may have one passion or many interests. When we do what we love to do, we merge with a wider energy. It invigorates us and moves us beyond ourselves.

If we love to garden, we join with the seasonal energy of the earth. If we love to read, we become caught up in the creative interaction between the writer's words and our own response. If we love to swim, run, dance or play tennis, our body bursts with the exuberance of its movement. When we do what we love to do, we are fully engaged with an energy that is spontaneous, instinctive and larger than our everyday consciousness.

We Have Fun

Enjoying life and having fun are spirituality in action. We enjoy life every day, and it's everyday living we enjoy. We enjoy the small pleasures in life and the big ones, too. We enjoy a simple dinner, we enjoy a great vacation. We laugh with ourselves, we laugh with others. Laughter is wonderful — it's high-kicking spiritual energy. Our laughter is never hurtful because it is always respectful, so it heals us and can help heal others, too. We learn that when things get tough, if we can find a reason to smile or even if we can smile without much reason, a good energy comes to us and gives us strength.

A gym teacher said, "When you think you can't lift your leg even one more time, forget your leg and smile." Just see what happens.

We Have Friends

No one heals alone. We all need the spiritual lift only the love of friends or family can give. Our responsibility is to reach out for it. This is something most of us do with great reluctance. We feel safer and more in control alone.

But as we overcome our reluctance, we find a world of help and understanding that comes from the energy of others. In *The Road Less Traveled*, M. Scott Peck defines love as "the will to extend one's self for the purpose of nurturing one's own or another's spiritual growth." To give and receive this love is why we have friends.

We Give And We Receive

Spiritual energy flows when we give time, attention and help to others. Spiritual energy continues to flow when we receive. It's spiritually strong to know that what we have to give is valuable. Asking for help when we need it requires spiritual strength, too. Giving and receiving attention and kindness creates a cycle of positive energy that never needs to end.

We Detach From Others' Opinions Of Us

Spiritual energy surges when we believe our *own* respectful, loving opinion of ourselves. This opinion is our truth. We need to detach quietly and firmly from the destructive messages of our past and from the negative messages we get from some of the people around us. We listen to the opinions of others, but then we realistically evaluate what they are telling us. We compare what we hear with our own truth and then accept or reject what the other person said. When we believe in our truth and harness it to the actions we take, we find a personal integrity that is infused with spiritual energy. And we heal.

We Say Affirmations

We become what we think we are — this self-fulfilling prophecy is a psychological truth. Affirmations can help us turn a negative self-fulfilling prophecy into a positive one. We state affirmations as positive truths about ourselves in the present. We say them as mantras when we get up in the morning, when we get into a tight spot or when we go to bed at night. We tape notes on the refrigerator door or the bathroom mirror: "I am courageous." "I am a great father." "I can." "Today I will act like a strong woman." "I am very good at what I do." "I feel serene as I work in the middle of chaos."

We can take snatches of inspiration from whatever we read or hear and make them our own. It doesn't matter where affirmations come from. We say them to ourselves and *listen*, we look at them and *see*. Then we begin to act on them. It just happens. The spiritual energy that lives deep inside of us hears the good thought and gives us strength to move.

We Meditate

To meditate is to switch mental gears. We stop whatever we are doing and sit quietly and comfortably. We consciously relax our muscles. We concentrate on breathing. We turn off both the mental babble inside our heads and the sounds and distractions around us. We don't make an effort to control what's going on. We empty our minds and our attitude becomes passive. We focus on an object, a sound, a word or an image — a neutral focus that keeps our mind from wandering. As thoughts and feelings drift across our mental landscape, we gently let them go without effort.

Meditation keeps us alert, yet gives us a deep emotional, mental and physical relaxation that refreshes us. Sometimes we hear messages that come from the deep center of our spirit. There's nothing mystic[1] about meditation — it's an innate state of being. It's healing and it just takes practice.

We Seek Guidance From Within

We reach beyond our *conscious* self for guidance. Seeking guidance involves putting aside our personal agenda with its rigid opinions and answers. We try to hear a new voice and make new mental and emotional connections. The new voice we hear when we seek guidance is the transcended part of ourselves. It comes from beyond the limits of our conscious personality and personal views. It's an inner voice that may come to us in meditation or prayer, or our transcended self may help us hear other people in a new way. Sometimes it appears as an odd, unsolicited thought or idea. It may speak loudly so we can't miss it or it may only whisper so at first we don't hear. Whenever it comes and however insistent it is, we must listen to this voice. If we trust it, it will never let us down. It is a spiritual resource we have *within* ourselves always. The only requirements are to be open, to hear and to accept.

Step 11 — What's The Outcome?

We Grow In Abiding Strength

As we practice and practice the Eleventh Step, our abiding strength becomes exercised and durable. We become increasingly well-stocked with strength and good feelings. We can compare it with a car battery. If we engage spiritual energy as we go about our lives, we stay charged up. If we sputter along in life, not really connecting with spiritual resources around us, our battery stays weak. If we become drained physically, mentally, or emotionally, we, like the car, simply quit. We must be careful not to get spiritually depleted. But if our battery does die out, we hook up to the Eleventh Step and recharge.

We Grow In Wisdom

Both self-knowledge and wisdom are important. Self-knowledge comes from our own thoughtful evaluation, and without it we couldn't discover who we are or decide how to change. But wisdom is something different. Wisdom comes through our spiritual connections, connections outside of our consciousness. It's wider and deeper than our conscious knowledge. It is non-judgmental and objective — it has no favorites, not even us. Wisdom comes through our open and quiet mind and tells us what we need to know, even when we don't want to hear it.

We Grow In Enjoyment Of Life

There's no doubt about it, the 12-Step way is a happy way to live. We learn to emphasize the present, to see an honest reality. We search for joy. We do things we love to do. We are open and curious. We make friends. Turmoil and pain disappear as we reclaim and rehabilitate our lives. Life actually gets to be fun.

---

*Engage spiritual energy and awareness
to help us grow in abiding strength and wisdom
and in the enjoyment of life.*

**Today I will enjoy life. I will choose and use
whatever strengthens me and nourishes my spirit.**

· CHAPTER THIRTEEN ·

Step 12

---

*Practice the principles of these
Steps in all our affairs and carry
the 12-Step message to others.*

Principles: Commitment, Self-discipline, Service to others

• • • • • •

Step 12 acts as an arrow, sending us right back into the entire program. As we "practice the principles of these Steps in all our affairs," we refer back again and again to the principles we have studied.

Insight	Self-examination
Honesty	Personal honesty
Hope	Self-acceptance
Faith	Personal integrity
Decision-making	Willingness to change

Acceptance	Personal responsibility
Action	Self-discipline
Humility	Service to others
Trust	Forgiveness
Courage	Perseverance
Compassion	Commitment to balance
Connection to spiritual resources	

One Day At A Time

Each morning we wake up to a new day — a day that will be full of choices. There will be big choices that we know will have an impact on our lives. There will be small choices that reinforce us, sustain us and ultimately create us. We are learning to make the choices that express the 12-Step principles. In themselves, the Steps and their principles are only printed words lying lifeless on a piece of paper. The trick is to decide what they mean to each of us and how to breathe life into them in our real world. Here are some examples.

• • • •

When I'm afraid, I can ask myself, "What is the courageous thing to do?" And maybe I can share my fear with a trusted friend.

When I'm full of rage, I can ask myself how to handle my anger so I'm respectful to myself and to the person I'm mad at.

When I've hurt someone, I can make an immediate and unconditional amend and then go on without guilt.

When I feel tired or depressed, I can look to my own special kind of spiritual help.

• • • •

Bringing the 12-Step principles to life is a continual process of learning to live with personal integrity. Unfortunately, we often fall short. We lie to keep the peace. We refuse to try a new way to do something, not because it's a bad idea but because it's different. We continue to carry a grudge. We're afraid to trust our friend.

These things happen, but it's important to keep our values and goals in front of us. This is the only way life will get better. If we keep remembering where we are trying to go and take responsibility for trying to get there, eventually we will.

As we practice the principles, we don't think of ourselves as bad people trying to become good. We've fought that battle for a long time and haven't made much progress. It's more helpful to look at the program as continual self-redemption, discovery and renewal — always hopeful, always open to another option and the spiritual resources around us. The 12 Steps can't turn us into "better" women and men, but they can make us more emotionally honest about who we are. They teach us that our integrity is not determined by what we say we believe. Our integrity is determined by what we understand about ourselves, what we do, how we actually live.

To Walk The Talk

We carry the 12-Step message to others by the way we live our lives. We don't have to talk about it or to proselytize. We can if we want to, but it isn't necessary. We don't have to be perfect in order to carry the message either. We just have to live with integrity.

When someone or something gives us a great spiritual gift, that gift can never really be repaid. There just isn't any way. But it can be passed on. The 12 Steps have offered us a gift. We have taken it. And we can offer it to others by our living example.

Now it's time to take ourselves — stronger, aware of what integrity means — and reach out to others. In the end this program is about reaching in and reaching out, stretching between our deepest self and the community and the natural world around us. What we need to understand is that the 12-Step program leads us into ourselves and outward to our universe. It's a kind of continuous homecoming — inward, outward, inward, outward — it doesn't matter. We are at home in ourselves and at home in the world. This is the promise that the Steps bring us to.

"But Dorothy, you *are* home," cries the Witch of the North. "All you have to do is wake up."

---

*Practice the principles of these Steps
in all our affairs and
carry the 12-Step message to others.*

**Today I will select one 12-Step principle
and consciously live
by it as I go through my day.**

· CHAPTER FOURTEEN ·

Groups: Shared Energy For Growth

Twelve-Step groups support us in our recovery. In them we identify with others who have problems similar to ours. We come together to share our common solution: the working of the Steps. We meet to talk, to gather insight and courage and to share our experiences.

Twelve-Step Groups Are A Different Kind Of Group

The method of a 12-Step group is not the same as the method of a typical support group or therapy group. In a 12-Step group each person works a self-directed program. There is no facilitator or professional leader. Members of the group focus on the process of the Steps and on their own recovery. The relationship among members is respectful, caring and impartial. Group members support each other as each person works to apply the 12-Steps to his or her life.

In contrast, support groups often resemble informal social groups and may or may not have a professional leader. Participants are likely to be actively involved with each other and with the group process. They talk about their current and past lives with feedback being an important part of the interaction.

Therapy groups are always led by a professional. Members work on their own issues with the involved support of other group members. The experience is often emotionally intense because the objective of therapy is to work with profound and powerful feelings. Some 12-Step members go to support or therapy groups. Either can complement, but not replace, the 12-Step group experience.

The Shared Solution Is More Important Than The Shared Problem

Twelve-Step groups often organize around a shared problem. Some of them are Overeaters Anonymous, Emotions Anonymous, Alcoholics Anonymous, Gamblers Anonymous, Narcotics Anonymous and Al-Anon for the families of alcoholics. Twelve-Step groups also support Adult Children of Alcoholics and people with Chronic Illness and Disabilities.

Whatever the shared problem of the group, it's the Steps that are the focus. The shared problem is only the starting point. This means that as time passes, group members are able to move beyond the problem that they all share and apply the Steps to many other areas of their lives.

For example, in an AA meeting, recovering alcoholics talk about their struggles with worry, anger, relationships, low self-esteem, compulsive overwork and other ongoing difficulties. Focusing on the Steps, they are slowly able to move beyond their alcoholism and expand the 12-Step solution to their other life-diminishing emotions and behaviors.

Groups Are Guided By The 12 Traditions

The 12 Traditions are to the health of the group what the Twelve Steps are to an individual's recovery. They were adopted by AA's first International Convention in 1950. Following are shortened and paraphrased versions of the 12 Traditions:

1. Common welfare comes first. Personal recovery depends on group unity.
2. Group conscience is the group's authority. Decisions are arrived at by group conscience. Minority ideas get thoughtful attention. Leaders themselves have no authority; they are trusted servants.
3. The only requirement for membership is to show up at a meeting. There are no other membership requirements, no rules and no dues.
4. Each group is autonomous. Its only responsibility is to work with the Steps and to follow the 12 Traditions.
5. Each group has one purpose: to be a support for recovering people.
6. Groups never endorse, finance or associate with outside related enterprises. There must be a clear boundary between 12-Step groups and programs, such as treatment facilities, counseling services, workshops, support groups and so on.
7. Every group is fully self-supporting, declining outside contributions. This keeps groups independent. Nonmembers may not donate money, goods or meeting space. A collection taken at meetings pays for rent and supplies.
8. Groups are non-professional. Service to the group is volunteer and is done without pay.
9. Organization within a group and among groups is kept to a minimum.
10. Groups have no opinion on outside issues. This neutrality on all issues keeps groups from being drawn into public controversy.
11. Public relations policy is based on *attracting* members to the program, rather than on *promoting* it. Member's anonymity is always maintained in the public eye and in the media.
12. Anonymity is the foundation of all the traditions. Groups are guided by the principles of the Steps, not by personalities.

A Simple Meeting Format And
Guidelines For Talking And Listening

The format is the basic structure of a meeting. It lets us know what to expect and when to expect it. Once a simple structure is established, anyone can step into the role of temporary leader.

The leader keeps the meeting within the format, but has no other role. The treasurer pays the rent and buys supplies for the group. Everyone shares responsibility. Members gladly take turns at service positions and other group duties.

The real business of the meeting is the mutual identification and support among members. Following is a commonly-used meeting format that makes good use of limited time. The guidelines for small group sharing ensure equality, respect and safety for all.

1. The leader opens the meeting on time. The affirmation of serenity is recited.
2. Five to ten minutes are taken for self-introductions, to greet newcomers, to read the 12 Steps, to take care of group business and for announcements. A donation basket is passed. A sign-up sheet for speaking at meetings may also be passed.
3. The person who has previously signed up for the meeting gives a short informal talk. The focus is usually one of the Steps. We talk about the realities of our actions, thoughts and emotions, about how we are using the particular Step in our lives and how our own 12-Step program is helping us. Speaking at a meeting is an opportunity for growth. The only feedback the speaker gets is a hearty "thank you" by the leader.
4. Before the meeting breaks into smaller groups, the leader may read this statement:

• • • •

The views heard in this meeting are those of the speaker. We each interpret and work the 12 Steps in our own way. In your small group, everyone will have a chance to speak without interruption. When people speak, we do not give feedback unless requested. We do not give advice. We take what we want from the meeting and leave the rest.

• • • •

5. The remainder of the time is spent in small groups where all members have the opportunity to talk and to hear what others have to say.

Group Process Is How We Talk And Listen

Twelve-Step groups must model health for the members. It is important that we don't engage in the same behavior we are trying to recover from. Without the use of clear guidelines, we are apt to lapse into old familiar patterns and the group may collapse under the weight of our combined confusion, anger and hurt.

Groups function well or poorly because of something called group process. Group process is simply how we talk and how we listen. When we take our turn to talk, we remember that our responsibility is to ourselves, not to other group members.

Using the 12 Steps as a guide, we talk about what we need to talk about. We talk about how we understand the particular Step being discussed and how we are using it in our current lives. We talk about a problem, our feelings, our actions and reactions. We talk about the new life options created by working the Steps and the additional problems our new options are creating. We don't need to have others agree with us or understand us. In fact, we don't even need to completely understand what we are saying ourselves. Confusion and strong feelings are always at home in meetings. They are a good sign that changes are happening. The understanding comes later as we continue to make progress in our program.

When others talk, we support, accept and love them by practicing large, spiritual listening. We put our own opinions, ideas and judgments aside. We listen with an open and relaxed acceptance of the person speaking and of what is being said. We don't evaluate or judge. Non-acceptance and judgment are the results of narrow, shallow listening. We know that any opinion we form is likely to apply only to ourselves. Large listening is called detached listening because it is detached from the personal limitations of our emotions, judgments and evaluations. Detached listening is an expression of spirituality and trust.

When we listen with open acceptance and non-evaluation, the speaker feels heard because the speaker *is* heard. Being heard and accepted without correction is something most of us have never experienced. The circle of safety created by respectful, emotionally neutral listeners enables us to say whatever we need or want to say, without fear of being put on the spot or fear of censure. Having others listen with an open, relaxed and neutral acceptance is a vote of confidence in our ability to work things out. Smiles and a few kind words provide human connection, warmth and caring.

We Each Have Different Ways Of Working

Interpretations and ways to work the 12 Steps vary widely among members, and our own interpretations and applications will change as time passes. The only concern we need to have is how *we* understand the Steps and how *we* will apply them to our lives today.

Within a group, members are in different phases of development and will focus on different issues. This mix works wonderfully. It means we can learn from each other. And it means we can learn tolerance and acceptance when our views are at odds. There's a humorous saying that the 12-Step program works as well for those who do it all wrong as it does for those who do it our way. That's true, it does.

The Look And Feel Of A Supportive Group

We want our groups to support growth in self-acceptance, personal change and happiness. Some groups do better at this than others. They are made up of people, and people are anything but perfect, so most groups are a mixed bag of dependable support and little irritations. The following are some positive things to look for:

1. The group is open. Newcomers are immediately welcomed and included. This is one of the best indicators of a supportive group.
2. The group feels like a safe place. We feel an emotional comfort within the group.
3. Group members share laughter, many smiles and sometimes tears. The emotions expressed are genuine and natural.
4. People are free to be as open or as private as they choose. Respect for privacy is crucial. There is no probing.
5. The group makes good use of time.
6. Everyone has equal status. Length of time in the group or 12-Step program doesn't confer special status or privilege.
7. There is a feeling of mutual respect. There is no competition among members.
8. It is not apparent which members have social or other connections outside of the group.
9. When members are having a hard time or are making decisions that may sabotage their recovery, the group doesn't interfere. Instead, other members smile and say, "Keep coming back." They greet returning members warmly.
10. Members work an active program in the group. Sometimes this looks like backsliding and confusion. There are no "presentations" of a polished program.
11. No feedback is given unless it is asked for.
12. The 12 Traditions are honored.

When We Each "Keep Coming Back"

Our group exists to support us in our recovery. Each of us is in charge of our own program and it's never the job of the group to direct us. We determine our own realities, our own directions, our own needs and the working of our own solutions. A healthy group will support us, no matter what our personal point of view, the issues we face, our personalities, who we are or what we have done. A healthy group simply helps us use the Steps.

Because of the practice of large, detached listening, we are able to support the recoveries of a wide range of people with differing points of view. Some of us are eccentric, some of us have painful issues that are difficult to talk about and difficult to hear about and some of us have checkered histories. Detached listening makes it possible for us to support each other when we are following divergent paths.

We believe we are each guided by individual inner strength and wisdom. Another person's inner strength and wisdom may look as if it needs some help. But we keep hands off and we practice trusting the spiritual strength of others. As we stay detached, we develop a deep respect and awe for each other's inner spiritual strength and wisdom. We learn to love each other in a large way, a new way that lies beyond personal likes and emotions. Large trust in other people's inner strength and large listening lead to large love among us. This is a miracle, and it can happen in a 12-Step group.

· CHAPTER FIFTEEN ·

How To Work
A Program

Our Program Is Our Personal Way Of Life

We create our own 12-Step program, every Step of the way. We create it piece by piece as we work our way through the Steps. Everyone's life and interpretation of the Steps is different, so each of us custom-makes a program to fit our own attitudes, beliefs, needs and desires.

It's important to understand that no matter how hard we work our program, it's going to take a long time for the things we learn from it to become automatic for us. Psychologists say it takes an average of six months before newly-learned behavior becomes really integrated into our thinking, and at least twice that long before we habitually use new behavior when we face a crisis. There is simply no quick fix. There is only commitment and practice.

In the beginning many of us approach the program in a deliberate and formal way. Some of us carry small cards with the Steps printed on them.

We take them out and use them as reminders whenever and wherever we need to. We do lots of ritual reading of Step literature. We talk to other people who are involved with the program. We think about what it means for us to "work a program" and our commitment deepens. Reading the Steps, thinking about them and consciously applying them, we gradually begin to take on the 12-Step way of life.

As time passes we get looser and more flexible in how we use the Steps. We start to realize that, although the cards, literature and other people can give us suggestions, only we can sift through all that material. Only we can mold it into our own wonderful, perfectly adapted program for living. Finally the 12 Steps and the principles behind them become our way of life, working deep into our belief system.

If we are truly committed to living within the framework of the Steps, if we do our very best to understand and use them, whatever we do in working our program will turn out to be exactly right for us. Even though we make what seem like mistakes, we learn from the experience and do better. Our mistakes actually become stepping stones. We learn that making a blunder isn't a catastrophe, it's a challenge — and out of that challenge we can jump ahead. In the past, mistakes were a reason for self-loathing. The Steps teach us that they can become a reason for growth and self-trust.

We Work A Selfish Program

"Selfish" is a really dirty word. Most people, particularly women, are brought up to "share," to "think of the other person first," to "not be selfish." So it's very hard to accept that in working a successful 12-Step program we must put ourselves first. It's an exercise in self-love. We must learn to take care of ourselves instead of taking care of other adults. (Children, of course, need parenting.)

We must learn to take care of ourselves instead of expecting or letting others take care of us. The 12-Step way teaches us self-love, self-trust and self-respect. Our self-ish program turns into a sharing one. In the past we haven't had the things the program teaches us, so we couldn't share them with anyone else. Our selfish program taught us to practice on ourselves. We did and now we can share loving, trusting and respectful relationships with people around us. Selfish becomes beautiful.

We Work A Practical Program

Our personal program must be realistic and concrete. An effective program is not a pie-in-the-sky scheme, nor is it set apart from our real daily lives. We don't try to live *up* to a mythical model, we bring the program *down* into our daily muddles and irritations. This is the only way to make change.

Our program is a bag of practical tools we carry with us. The tools include the Steps, principles, slogans, affirmations and anything else that helps. *Every* time we face a difficulty, we take out our bag and pull out what we need. *Every* time, *every* day. As beginners we'll probably be clumsy. Whatever tools we use, we'll strain too hard or not hard enough. Then we'll begin to get the feel of it and use our tools with ease and mastery. Finally we don't even have to reach for them, they simply become an integral part of the way we are in the world.

We Work A Focused Program

Unfortunately, we can't change all at once. We keep our program manageable by focusing on a few thoughts, feelings or behaviors at a time. We think about what we can do today. Long-term goals are invaluable. We have to have them to help set our direction and act as beacons that guide us and hold us on course. But it's our short-term goals that move us along. Short-term goals, successfully accomplished, add up to big progress — they are the way our program lives.

So we focus on short periods of time. One goal after another, one day, one hour, one minute at a time. If we concentrate only on the big picture, we feel frustrated and helpless, but we learn we can do almost anything for just a little while. For just a little while we can accomplish what we can't even imagine doing for a lifetime. Of course we plan ahead, but the program teaches us we can't control tomorrow and living well today is the very best preparation for the future.

Every day we ask ourselves, "What am I working on today?" Then we have our daily assignment. For example, today we may focus on our tendency to "help" our teenage daughter by pointing out her errors and telling her how to correct them. Our assignment is to notice when we get the urge to do this and to stop. Just for today.

Just for today we will give up our role as overbearing teacher/perfectionist/parent. When she makes a mistake or is about to make one, we will practice a loving detached silence or friendly neutral banter or upbeat encouragement. If we can't do this for a whole day, maybe we can do it for an hour — if an hour seems like an eternity, 15 minutes is progress.

It's discouraging to have the landscape littered with dozens of unfinished assignments lying around. So at first it's best to focus on only one or two goals. When we are new at this, we need plenty of time to prepare a plan and carry it out. Then we give ourselves lots of congratulations when we succeed, or we regroup and replan when we fail. Later when the Steps have become our way of living, we can include many more goals. But the short-term focus still holds. We live one minute, one hour, one day at a time. For the rest of our lives we may look toward the future, but today is when we live.

We Work A Steady Program

Desire produces commitment, commitment produces practice, practice produces consistency. The longer we work our program, the more it takes on a consistent steadiness. Steadiness shows in the consistency of effort, not necessarily in smoothness or outcome. A successful program lives and a living program changes.

When we work with the Steps, we change. Our interpretations, attitudes, beliefs, needs, focus and approach change and keep on changing. Change is renewal. We keep moving forward with steadiness — creating new goals, meeting them, failing, trying again and succeeding.

How Does A Group Fit In?

Some people work a program without attending meetings. Some people attend meetings and don't work a program. Most of us integrate group meetings into our programs, and attending them usually helps. Weekly meetings can have a very special place in our recovery. They can support us and keep us focused on the Steps. They can remind us to be selfish, practical and steady. A group also reminds us to have sponsors. Some sponsors help us for a short time, others serve us for years. Mainly they teach by example, but we talk to them, too. They are more experienced with the Steps than we are, they are farther along in their journey and they are invaluable for leading, helping or shoving us over the humps in our own program.

The Only Way To Make It Is To Work It

The only way we make ourselves and our lives better is to take action and to do the work. We can't just *think* a program, we have to *act* it. An overweight, overwrought doctor can explain the benefits of good food and exercise to us in perfect detail and with expert understanding. But all we have to do is look at him to know he doesn't experience what he is talking about. This doctor is a good role model for how *not* to work a 12-Step program. The details of our program may not be perfect, and we certainly aren't experts at understanding it. But we consistently study the Steps, think about them and act. The doctor can talk and talk and stay overweight and overstressed, but we act and act and become spiritually lean and serene.

· CHAPTER SIXTEEN ·

The Ongoing Journey

Our journey begins with birth and ends with death. It's a journey we're all going to take. There is no other way. Some of us haven't been comfortable or satisfied with the way our trip is going. We have been uneasy and in pain. Our spirits are hungry; their hunger shows in anxiety, depression, compulsive feelings and thoughts and actions. So we look for something to help us. Some of us choose a 12-Step program, and when we do, our journey becomes all we could hope for.

In the beginning we work hard at the program. We read each Step, study it, think about it and practice making the Steps our response of choice. We do this for months, perhaps for years, until the ways of the 12 Steps truly become ours. The Steps teach us many things — ways to think, ways to feel, ways to act. And they lead us home to our spiritual self. We learn to know this self, respect this self, trust this self and accept it as our own. We are no longer off-center, but settled in the center of who we truly are — and our centered self finds its place in the whole of the universe.

We become people who travel our journey searching out peace and joy and dealing with pain as it comes along, instead of people who live with pain and grab whatever little pieces of joy and serenity come their way.

In Chapter One of this book we said each person is like a kaleidoscope, that our physical, emotional and mental components continually rearrange themselves. What we didn't say is that these parts are continually reforming around a still, unmoving center. But they are. The 12-Step journey is a spiritual quest that leads to the core of self, to the center of the kaleidoscope. Here is where our own personal 12-Steps have led.

ARLYS

"We are not human beings having a spiritual experience, but spiritual beings having a human experience." This idea from the popular author Wayne Dyer is true for me. I have always been a free spirit, a regular flower child in temperament. I have always had an affinity for fairy tales, visualization, artsy stuff and intuitive thinking. However, I lacked practical living skills. I didn't know how to protect myself from others, from their actions and their judgments of me. I didn't know I could set goals for myself and act on them. I didn't know that my normal human needs were okay. I didn't know I wasn't selfish and bad for asking for what I needed. In short, I didn't know how other human beings lived. I only guessed.

In the 12-Step program I have made some progress toward being a normal human being, at least normal for me. I have connected myself to everyday life in normal ways. I still love fairy tales and artsy stuff, but now I am much more than a free spirit. I am centered in a real life. I have goals. I have needs that I meet. I have responsibilities that matter to me and others. I can act. I am competent. I am a more balanced person, living a real life in the here and now. My spirituality is richer and fuller as a result.

Working with the 12 Steps has been a continual homecoming for me. Because I was never "at home" in my own humanity, I felt a deep longing, like being overcome with homesickness. I searched for answers in all sorts of places, but nothing outside of me brought me peace. I remained sick at heart. I thought there was something seriously wrong with me, and there was. I was longing for my Self, and my Self was longing for a home. In my program I set about finding my Self and giving my Self a home within my life. I discovered pieces of myself, real treasures, and brought them home to live in me. Little by little, I found pieces and fit them together inside just right to be Me. I discovered and constructed my own humanity.

These are a few of the many things I've learned about myself:

1. I am strong. I have learned that as others have hurt me, I also have the power to hurt others. In fact, I have great power to destroy. I also have great power for good. In days of yore I thought of myself as benign and harmless. I thought I wasn't capable of hurting others, that it simply wasn't in my nature. I also liked to think I was too weak to effectively change my life. In my program I have come to know my own power and inner strength. I have as much personal power as anyone in the world. I have all the inner strength I need.

2. I have learned detachment. I began by detaching from the actions of the alcoholic in my life. I learned to act, to live my own life rather than to react to others. My skill in detachment has led me to know about love.

3. I know about love. It is a mysterious contradiction in my 12-Step program. Personal love is my attachment to another. But sometimes I get a brief glimpse of a larger love, an unconditional love that goes beyond the personal. I experience this larger love when I am willing to release my attachments, beginning with my attachment to myself. This larger love is total detachment, total acceptance and an absolute absence of judgment. I can't grasp this love or work toward it. I wouldn't even want it for a long period of time, because I like my everyday life in the here and now.

4. I have clear boundaries. This is the nuts and bolts of my program. I know where I stop and where others begin. I know what is mine to change and what is none of my business. This is some of what I know about boundaries:

- I do not carry the feelings of other people, and I do not project my feelings onto others.
- I let others suffer their own pain. I do not rescue or have answers for them.
- I ask for what I need and do not let others give me what I do not want, whether it is answers or things.
- I do not let others take from me, but I choose what I want to give.
- I make conscious decisions about my time, my money, my talents, my actions, my feelings.
- I speak only for myself. No one else can speak for me or define me.

5. I accept who I am. For instance, I am basically a loner. I like people, but I need lots of quiet time by myself. I have accepted this, not as a personal shortcoming, but as a positive part of who I am.

6. I am a good person. I am not perfect, but I am basically good. I am respectful of others and I am a safe person to be around.

My approach to the Steps is basically pragmatic. I have seen that success with the 12 Steps has more to do with what a person does than what a person believes about god. I think of the Steps as my program in self-management. They have given me a systematic way to develop useful skills in living. This does not mean the Steps are surface exercises in self-improvement. For me, they have been a way to develop my humanity and integrate it into a balanced way of life.

MARTHA

From the time I was 12 years old I was fascinated by human psychology. I had a passionate interest in other people's mental processes and in my own. As the years passed, what I learned became the basis of how I approached life — it was no surprise that I ended up as a clinical psychologist. My life evolved. I was pretty comfortable and competent with myself, my family, friends and profession. Then I fell through to another layer.

I wanted to retire. I had physical and emotional reasons to move on to a new phase in life. And I couldn't. I just couldn't stop working. I used all my old methods of figuring myself out, I'd get a lot of fancy answers — and keep on working.

One day as I was watching the first winter goldfinches at the feeder, an unexpected thought turned my attention inward. I realized I had the unshakeable belief that if I weren't doing work society defined as productive, I had no right to live. My productive body had a place in the world, but my self, my single spirit, didn't. A dear friend and colleague said it was time I stopped playing around the edges of the 12-Step program, and began to honestly come to grips with it. So I did.

I came to this program as both a psychologist and an atheist. Steps 4 through 12 are action Steps. All my professional training and life experience made these Steps easy for me to accept. They made good sense intellectually, psychologically and emotionally. They acted as a useful, friendly framework for me to refer to.

Steps 1 through 3 were something else. Early in life I seriously questioned the Episcopal church in which I was raised and rejected much of its doctrine. In high school and college I took classes in comparative religion and questioned more and more. My searching led me to total confusion — I equated spirituality with organized religion and rejected both. I talked about being an atheist, and my friends said, "You can't be an atheist and still be such a spiritual person." I just didn't get it, so I decided the whole thing was irrelevant to my life.

But in the end, of course, it wasn't. As I stood deep in my middle years I had to begin the struggle to understand my own spirituality. I had to search deeply and honestly, to overcome old messages and biases, to be humble and to accept my strength. This is some of what I've learned.

My old hibiscus plant was my first teacher. It taught me about the affirmation of serenity. Early one dark winter morning I was sitting quietly enjoying the stillness and peace before the beginning of my very active day. My mind was drifting, thinking about powerlessness and spiritual resources that were beyond my conscious control.

How could I *ever* accept these ideas? How could I *ever* work with the 12-Step program? I glanced out of the window. It was snowing. Huge flakes drifted down in the lamplight reflected on the snowy ground outside. My glance fell on my old hibiscus plant, dearly loved, proudly presenting me with its daily gift of a glorious red blossom. The flower was wonderful, but the plant was lopsided and stringy. I knew I should cut it back, allowing it to start new growth near its base, but I was afraid it would never regain the power to bloom. How could I stand to lose the pleasure and strength those flowers gave me?

Suddenly a thought flew into my consciousness. I could do the best thing for my plant — I could give it a chance for new life. But in order to do that, I would have to surrender the outcome. I would need determination, commitment, hope, faith, willingness to risk and patience. I would have to accept that I had no control over whether I would ever see my hibiscus bloom again. I could do everything within my power. I could give it light, food, water and loving care, but that was *all* I could do.

My old hibiscus taught me the lesson of the Serenity Affirmation and the first three Steps. It taught me to accept that there are things I cannot change, that the outcome is simply beyond my control. It taught me that I need to reach for the courage to change the things I can. I trimmed my plant.

Since that morning I've learned a lot of other things about my spiritual self and the program will teach me many more in the years ahead. These are the spiritual messages that seem most important to me today:

1. I've always made what I now accept as spiritual connections, but before my struggle with the Steps I wouldn't identify those things as spiritual. I was too proud. Now I accept and am openly grateful for all of the wonderful ways I gain support from spiritual resources beyond myself.

2. Serenity and spiritual fulfillment are not Huge Happenings. They come from stringing together little moments, sometimes milli-seconds of peace, joy, strength, hope and faith. I acknowledge them, accept them, put them in the bank and accumulate spiritual wealth.

3. Spiritual resources are not just for hard times. I use them every day, in good times and in bad. They enrich me when my life is wonderful and support me when it's cruel.

4. Pain doesn't last forever. I can bear it and it will pass. I can always make my own kind of spiritual connections to help myself endure.

5. Whatever path my life takes provides me with the opportunity for spiritual growth. This is true whether it's a path of joy, hard labor or sorrow — I can use any experience to strengthen my spirit.

6. Faith and Grace are beautiful words. I don't have to tie them to religion. Faith provides my spirit with constant, consistent, day-to-day energy. The force of Grace, of unseen helping hands, supports me and enriches my life. Grace touches me when I am open and aware of the ever-present spiritual resources lying beyond my limited consciousness.

7. Joy gives fire to my spirit. It's a personal explosion deep within my physical body. It comes when I allow myself, just for a moment, to become truly connected with the radiant blossom on my newly grown hibiscus.

·APPENDIX A·

The 12 Steps

A Nontheistic Translation

1. Admit we are powerless over other people, random events and our own persistent negative behaviors, and that when we forget this, our lives become unmanageable.

   Principles: Insight, Honesty

2. Came to believe that spiritual resources can provide power for our restoration and healing.

   Principles: Hope, Faith

3. Make a decision to be open to spiritual energy as we take deliberate action for change in our lives.

   Principles: Decision, Acceptance, Action

4. Search honestly and deeply within ourselves to know the exact nature of our actions, thoughts and emotions.
   Principles: Self-examination, Personal honesty, Self-acceptance

5. Will talk to another person about our exact nature.
   Principles: Trust, Personal integrity

6. Be entirely ready to acknowledge our abiding strength and release our personal shortcomings.
   Principle: Willingness to change

7. Work honestly, humbly and courageously to develop our assets and to release our personal shortcomings.
   Principles: Personal responsibility, Involvement in change, Courage, Humility, Self-discipline

8. List all people we have harmed, including ourselves, and be willing to make amends to them all. Be willing to forgive those who have harmed us.
   Principles: Compassion, Personal honesty and Accountability

9. Whenever possible, we will carry out unconditional amends to those we have hurt, including ourselves, except when to do so would cause harm.
   Principles: Compassion, Change, Honesty and Responsibility, Forgiveness, Self-discipline

10. Continue to monitor ourselves, to acknowledge our successes and quickly correct our lapses and errors.
    Principles: Perseverance, Integrity

11. Increasingly engage spiritual energy and awareness to continue to grow in abiding strength and wisdom and in the enjoyment of life.
    Principles: Openness, Connection to life and spiritual resources

12. Practice the principles of these Steps in all our affairs and carry the 12-Step message to others.
    Principles: Commitment, Self-discipline, Service to others.

The Twelve Steps are adapted with permission of Alcoholics Anonymous World Services, Inc. Please see page iv for original steps and further information.

·RESOURCES·

Secular Recovery Organizations

Rational Recovery
— affiliated with American Humanist Assoc.
7 Harwood Drive
P.O. Box 146
Amherst, N.Y. 14226-0146

R.R. is a self-help program in which participants attend group meetings once or twice a week for about a year. Group members share their experiences with addiction, and anonymity is respected. R.R. believes that alcohol and drug use is a personal problem that can be treated in a finite period of time, using the Rational Emotive therapy of Albert Ellis. The system helps members to root out irrational thoughts and beliefs that keep them from reaching their goal of freedom from addiction.

Secular Organizations for Sobriety
P.O. Box 15781
North Hollywood, CA 91615-5781

S.O.S. is an autonomous, non-profit, non-religious, non-professional group of sober alcoholics and addicts involved in a rational process of recovery. Anonymity is respected. Members maintain sobriety as a separate issue from religion or spirituality. S.O.S. proposes a healthy skepticism and encourages use of scientific evidence and rational materials available on the disease of alcoholism and addiction. Members believe that recovery is based on individual responsibility.

Women for Sobriety
P.O. Box 618
Quakertown, PA 18951
800-333-1606

W.F.S. proposes a "New Life" program for all recovering women with a sincere desire to change their lives. In group meetings women recover through the discovery of Self, gained by sharing experiences, hopes and encouragement with other women in like circumstances. W.F.S. is based on positive thinking, metaphysics, meditation, group dynamics and pursuit of health through nutrition. Anonymity is respected.

Helpful 12-Step Books from . . .
Health Communications

12 STEPS TO SELF-PARENTING For Adult Children
Philip Oliver-Diaz, M.S.W., and Patricia A. O'Gorman, Ph.D.
This gentle 12-Step guide takes the reader from pain to healing and self-parenting, from anger to forgiveness, and from fear and despair to recovery.
ISBN 0-932194-68-0 $7.95

SELF-PARENTING 12-STEP WORKBOOK: Windows To Your Inner Child
Patricia O'Gorman, Ph.D., and Philip Oliver-Diaz, M.S.W.
This workbook invites you to become the complete individual you were born to be by using visualizations, exercises and experiences designed to reconnect you to your inner child.
ISBN 1-55874-052-X $9.95

THE 12-STEP STORY BOOKLETS
Mary M. McKee
Each beautifully illustrated booklet deals with a step, using a story from nature in parable form. The 12 booklets (one for each step) lead us to a better understanding of ourselves and our recovery.
ISBN 1-55874-002-3 $8.95

VIOLENT VOICES:
12 Steps To Freedom From Emotional And Verbal Abuse
Kay Porterfield, M.A.
By using the healing model of the 12 Steps emotionally abused women are shown how to deal effectively with verbal and psychological abuse and to begin living as healed and whole people.
ISBN 1-55874-028-7 $9.95

GIFTS FOR PERSONAL GROWTH & RECOVERY
Wayne Kritsberg
A goldmine of positive techniques for recovery (affirmations, journal writing, visualizations, guided meditations, etc.), this book is indispensable for those seeking personal growth.
ISBN 0-932194-60-5 $6.95

3201 S.W. 15th Street,
Deerfield Beach, FL 33442-8190
1-800-851-9100

Health
Communications, Inc.®

New Books . . .
from Health Communications

HEAL YOUR SELF-ESTEEM: Recovery From Addictive Thinking
Bryan Robinson, Ph.D.

Do you have low self-esteem? Do you blame others for your own unhappiness? If so, you may be an addictive thinker. The 10 Principles For Healing, an innovative, positive approach to recovery, are integrated into this book to provide a new attitude with simple techniques for recovery.

ISBN 1-55874-119-4 $9.95

HEALING ENERGY: The Power Of Recovery
Ruth Fishel, M.Ed., C.A.C.

Linking the newest medical discoveries in mind/body/spirit connections with the field of recovery, this book illustrates how to balance ourselves mentally, physically and spiritually to overcome our addictive behavior.

ISBN 1-55874-128-3 $9.95

CREDIT, CASH AND CO-DEPENDENCY: The Money Connection
Yvonne Kaye, Ph.D.

Co-dependents and Adult Children seem to experience more problems than most as money can be used as an anesthetic or fantasy. Yvonne Kaye writes of the particular problems the co-dependent has with money, sharing her own experiences.

ISBN 1-55874-133-X $9.95

THE LAUNDRY LIST: The ACoA Experience
Tony A. and Dan F.

Potentially The Big Book of ACoA, *The Laundry List* includes stories, history and helpful information for the Adult Child of an alcoholic. Tony A. discusses what it means to be an ACoA and what the self-help group can do for its members.

ISBN 1-55874-105-4 $9.95

LEARNING TO SAY NO: Establishing Healthy Boundaries
Carla Wills-Brandon, M.A.

If you grew up in a dysfunctional family, establishing boundaries is a difficult and risky decision. Where do you draw the line? Learn to recognize yourself as an individual who has the power to say no.

ISBN 1-55874-087-2 $8.95

3201 S.W. 15th Street,
Deerfield Beach, FL 33442-8190
1-800-851-9100

Health
Communications, Inc.®